Other Routes: Part-time Higher Education Policy

THE CUTTING EDGE

Series Editors:
Malcolm Tight, Senior Lecturer in Continuing Education, University of Warwick.
Susan Warner Weil, Associate Director of Higher Education for Capability, the RSA.

This series deals with critical issues and significant developments in continuing education, focusing on its impact on higher education.

Current titles in the series:

Tom Bourner *et al.*: *Part-time Students and their Experience of Higher Education*
David Smith and Michael Saunders: *Other Routes: Part-time Higher Education Policy*

Other Routes: Part-time Higher Education Policy

DAVID M. SMITH AND
MICHAEL R. SAUNDERS

The Society for Research into Higher Education
& Open University Press

Published by SRHE and
Open University Press
Celtic Court
Buckingham
MK18 1XT

and

1900 Frost Road, Suite 101
Bristol, PA 19007, USA

First published 1991

British Library Cataloguing in Publication Data

Smith, David M.
    Other routes: part-time higher education policy.
    1. England. Higher education institutions. Part time courses.
    I. Title   II. Saunders, Michael R.
    378.42

    ISBN 0 335 15199 X
    ISBN 0 335 15198 1 (pbk)

Library of Congress Cataloging-in-Publication Data

Smith, David M. (David Michael), 1945–
    Other routes: part-time higher education policy / by David M. Smith and Michael
    R. Saunders.
        p.   cm.
    Includes bibliographical references (p.   ) and index.
    ISBN 0-335-15199-X (hard) ISBN 0-335-15198-1 (pbk.)
    1. Education, Higher–Great Britain. 2. Students, Part-time–Great Britain.
    I. Saunders, Michael R. (Michael Robert), 1942–   II. Title.
    LA637.S6 1991
    378.41—dc20   90-14160 CIP

Typeset by Rowland Phototypesetting Ltd
Bury St Edmunds, Suffolk
Printed in Great Britain by
St Edmundsbury Press Ltd, Bury St Edmunds, Suffolk

To our wives Susan and Clare

Contents

List of Figures and Tables

List of Figures and Table

Series Editor's Introduction

Other Routes: Part-time Higher Education Policy is one of the first books to be published in a new Society for Research into Higher Education/Open University Press series, *The Cutting Edge*. This series seeks to address the critical issues, and report upon significant research and development activity, at the cutting edge of continuing higher education.

The Cutting Edge series is based on the premiss that social, demographic, economic and technological trends are now combining to ensure that virtually all institutions of higher education are concerned to open up their provision to new kinds of students. It is highly appropriate that this book should be one of the first published in the series, therefore, since part-time routes have been one of the major growth areas of British higher education over the last two decades.

In this book, David Smith and Michael Saunders of Middlesex Polytechnic focus on the developing role of part-time first degree provision in the British higher education system. They both analyse its policy context and, using the results of recent survey work, examine many of the details of practice.

Smith and Saunders place their analysis within the context of the continuing tensions between the 'social democratic' and 'neo-liberal' perspectives on educational policy, the former dominant in the 1960s, the latter in the 1980s. Many of the current debates about aspects of higher education policy – e.g. access, credit transfer, distance learning, performance indicators – are fruitfully examined in the light of these tensions.

Interleaved with the policy analysis is an empirical study of the structure and funding of part-time degree courses. Smith and Saunders provide valuable data on the nature and size of these courses, on the progress and survival of the students enrolled in them, and on the quality of the results which they achieve. They consider the costing and financing of part-time degree courses, concluding that in most cases the staff involved are unaware of the costs and that most courses are funded on the traditional basis of 'departmental fudge'. The possible implications of changes in the methodology of higher education funding are then examined.

Smith and Saunders conclude by advocating, 'passionately, . . . that part-time higher education is taken seriously in policy debate'. This book represents both a substantial contribution to that debate *and* a useful means for structuring and understanding other contributions.

Other Routes: Part-time Higher Education Policy can be read in conjunction with two other books recently published by the Society for Research into Higher Education/Open University Press. One of these – *Part-time Students and their Experience of Higher Education*, by Tom Bourner, Andy Reynolds, Mahmoud Hamed and Ron Barnett – has been published simultaneously in *The Cutting Edge* series. This provides a detailed analysis of the characteristics, motivations and experiences of part-time first degree students in polytechnics and colleges. The second book – *Higher Education: A Part-time Perspective*, by myself – was published last year. It offers a comprehensive analysis of the nature and value of all forms and levels of part-time higher education in the United Kingdom, placing it in a historical and comparative context.

Malcolm Tight

Acknowledgements

Our thanks are due to a number of people for assisting us with this book. Malcolm Tight must especially be thanked, not only for his role as friendly and hard working editor of the series but also for the interest he has shown in this project from its inception and for the constructive way in which he has led debates about part-time issues in the press and in the Association for Part-time Higher Education. Keith Drake, Jim Gallacher, Jim Leahy, Harry Mitchell, Norman Sharp and David Watson all offered criticism on aspects of the work. At CNAA Nigel Nixon, Philip Jones and Ron Barnett were all very helpful both in terms of encouragement and constructive, often detailed, criticism. At Middlesex we have been influenced through debate with members of the Centre for Community Studies, the School of Sociology and Social Policy and the Academic Development Unit. We would particularly like to thank Geoff Dench, Joel Gladstone, Ted Lewis and Roger Harris as well as our many part-time students. We have also benefited from numerous discussions with our colleagues in the Association for Part-time Higher Education, especially Ron Bishop, Roger Fieldhouse, Dorothy Goldman, Ann Hanson, Peter Lewis and John Wakeford.

Frances Cohen, our part-time research assistant on a number of projects, assisted with the collection of some of the data. We are also indebted to Marilyn Tuson, Pam Atkinson and Susan Smith all of whom helped with typing and/or the preparation of graphs, tables and diagrams.

The research underlying this book was financially supported by a grant from CNAA Development Services. However, its initiation and the earlier data collection was financed by two small grants by Middlesex Polytechnic Faculty of Social Science. Some of the interviews with members of the panel were conducted while David Smith was a Research Officer at the Institute of Community Studies, Bethnal Green. We are grateful to all of these.

Chapter 2 uses material which has been previously published in an article in *Higher Education Review*, Vol. 20, No. 2, 1988. Part of Chapter 3 contains material which has been published in *Open Learning*, Vol. 4, No. 3, November 1989.

1 | Introduction

Aims and method

The aim of this book is to relate our detailed observations of the operation of part-time provision to key policy issues in higher education. Part-time higher education covers a broad spectrum, ranging from postgraduate programmes through first degree, diploma and professional courses to a variety of sub-degree work, as well as many courses which offer no formal qualifications. Our analysis concentrates particularly upon part-time first degree level provision because that has become a key area of policy debate in respect of the proposed expansion of higher education provision, the widening of educational opportunities and the impact of government proposals to modify the mandatory grant system with a system of loans for full-time students. The recent interest in part-time higher education has seen the production of studies describing the distribution of part-time provision (Tight 1982; Tight 1986), discussing different methods of presentation and delivery (Lewis 1988; Education Development Group 1990) or offering specific examples of practice (Johnson and Hall 1985; Gallacher, Leahy and Sharp 1986). These studies have undoubtedly been of value to practitioners and to educational administrators. However, there has been a tendency to deal with part-time provision as a self-contained entity. Our approach is different in that we wish to locate our practical concerns within a wider educational and policy context.

The growth in numbers and status of part-time routes into higher education raises questions about its relationship to a rapidly changing system of higher education. This has led us to explore the underlying factors promoting changes in the system and their possible effects on the prospects for part-time higher education provision. This dynamic relationship between part-time provision and the wider system of which it is an integral part is analysed within a framework drawn from political economy.

The empirical material used in this book derives from three sources. We conducted a national survey of part-time degree provision during the academic year 1985–86. While there has been an increase in student numbers since that time and some improvement in the level of financing part-time provision in polytechnics and colleges, these data remain relevant. Where there have been changes we indicate these in the text. This survey was followed up with a panel study of selected institutions, consisting of seven polytechnics, three universities, two colleges of higher education, one Scottish central institution and one college specializing in correspondence work. The purpose of the panel was to enable us to follow up issues of practice raised in the national survey and to look in depth at how policy is developed and responded to at a local level. The third source of material consists of official statistics, policy documents, internal statistics and documentation from the providing institutions as well as relevant research produced by academic establishments and interest groups. We also obtained information from interviews and conversations with a variety of policy makers in national government, educational quangos and at the local institutional level.

The structure of the book

The structure of this book reflects our intention of balancing the discussion of policy issues with detailed information about practice. In Chapter 2 we present some key policy debates on which much of the subsequent discussion is based, looking at factors in the political economy that are forcing changes upon the system of higher education. The era of post-war expansion, which produced the stable system of the 1960s (which we call the social democratic era) is contrasted with the more market-oriented contemporary approach (which we term neo-liberalism) which has challenged previous arrangements. This challenge has come in part from the interpretation of demographic changes and manpower requirements which has raised issues about the size and cost of the system and of its relevance. This in turn has led to a questioning of the degree of openness and accessibility of the system itself, as well as a re-evaluation of the place of continuing education within it. Towards the end of the chapter the growth and distribution of part-time provision is plotted in terms of current policy debates.

The next two chapters look in detail at two key aspects of degree level part-time provision. In Chapter 3 a model of two possible modes of provision – conventional and continuing – is presented and applied to part-time higher education. An analysis of the structure of available part-time provision is offered. Different types of part-time opportunities related to issues of access are identified. We are also concerned with the progress and survival of cohorts on part-time programmes and the 'quality' of the graduates produced.

Chapter 4 presents an analysis of the ways in which part-time higher education is financed by the providing institutions and by the state. Within the present system of funding higher education four models are identified which are used by institutions as the basis of funding their part-time provision. These are related to the methodologies employed by institutions to assess their course costings and in so doing evaluate how expensive they perceive their part-time degree level provision to be. The focus then shifts to the consequences of adopting different institutional funding models, firstly upon policy and planning within the institutions and then on the likely impact of national policies. Finally we consider the probable consequences of proposed changes in the structure of the financing of higher education and in particular the consequences of changes in fee income and the introduction of top-up loans.

In Chapter 5 we return to wider policy issues, locating the organization of part-time higher education, along with continuing education, in the wider organization of higher education. The organization of learning is seen not merely as a set of administrative arrangements but rather as the product of complex professional negotiations taking place within institutional cultures which face external social and political pressures. In the later part of the chapter we use our own empirical observations to look at the effects on part-time provision of adopting a specific set of organizational practices.

The final chapter briefly considers some of the continuing developments in higher education and their implications for part-time provision. In doing so we are aware that in the near future some of these issues may be superseded and perhaps resolved. Even so, we ask the reader to consider in cases where there appears to have been a solution how it came about and how it relates to the different educational models and policies described in this book. Finally we draw conclusions and consider the future prospects for part-time higher education.

2 | The Drive for Reform: Prospects for Access and Continuing Education

Higher education is being driven by several conflicting forces towards a reassessment of its practices and objectives. There are now a number of fissures in the educational consensus which emerged in the early 1960s and which to date has provided the rationale for the structure of British higher education. After decades of stability the system is being jolted by financial restraint and by the new and at times contradictory demands made upon it. In this chapter we attempt to connect the diverse factors which combine to produce pressure for reform and to signpost the directions which this might take. We are concerned particularly with how political changes and demographic and economic trends provide possibilities for extending continuing education through the development of part-time provision.

The era of social democratic expansion

The current organization of higher education is largely based upon the Robbins objectives of increasing access to both vocational and liberal education and ensuring initiation into a common culture and common standards of citizenship (Robbins 1963). The Robbins proposals were part of series of educational reforms undertaken within the assumptions and commitments of a wider political economy now termed Keynesian social democracy (Heald 1983; Marquand 1988). The general policy objective, informed by social science research and matched by increased public expenditure, was to expand educational opportunity throughout the system (Centre for Contemporary Cultural Studies 1981). Organizational changes and expansion undertaken within this framework were as much about social engineering and economic policy as about educational principles. Those principles were drawn from wider social objectives exemplified in the works of Crosland (1956) and Vaizey (1962).

The Robbins Committee's approach to the expansion of access to higher education was founded on the key distributional principle that 'Courses of higher education should be available for all those who are qualified by ability and attainment to pursue them and wish to do so' (Robbins 1963). By concentrating on the supply of places it omitted questions about what was being supplied. Robinson (1988) argues that it failed to address fundamental questions about the nature of a degree, the time and method of study and the place of research in relation to teaching within the universities. He also queries the place of GCE 'A' level as a suitable preparation for higher education.

In fact the expansion of higher education has been slow and limited in comparison with the achievements of other countries (Department of Education and Science 1985b; Department of Education and Science 1987b), with the participation rate of home students now standing at just over 14 per cent (Department of Education and Science 1988b). Even so, the means adopted for achieving this limited expansion – 'qualification by ability attainment' (in practice 'A' levels) and mandatory financial support for full-time students – appear relatively expensive. The system of mandatory grants, defended by the National Union of Students and the Labour Party as ensuring access, has achieved only a 7 per cent participation rate in the universities by socio-economic groups IV and V (i.e.: the working class).

The American educational commentator Martin Trow sees the British education system as locked in the 'Robbins cage', which, he argues, calls for the opening up of the system while simultaneously defending its special (exclusive) character (Trow 1988). Trow draws our attention to the characteristics of exclusion: the need to keep people out in order to maintain 'standards of excellence' and a superiority which is not just intellectual but also social. Increasing access would dilute the social cachet of a degree. If education is to be 'higher', it must be 'rare'. It also has to command respect for its authority. This attitude is, he argues, the basis of the demand for autonomy and academic freedom for its guardians, the academics.

Any political attempt to expand or alter the form of the system must address the assumptions embedded within it. Until recently alternatives to the conventional position, like part-time routes, were not taken seriously. A conservative theme informed the Robbins Committee and its recommendations, running parallel to its desire to increase access. Within the Social Democratic framework the emphasis was less upon seriously addressing the underlying bases of social inequality than upon compensating individuals whose market position adversely affected their ability to consume. This 'consumption politics' led to education concentrating on supply side issues without ever asking fundamental questions of the education system itself. Neither the product (education) nor its objectives were ever in doubt.

Alternatives to the conventional position have their roots in the pre-Robbins era (Kelly 1970). Less than a century ago part-time students constituted the majority outside Oxbridge and Durham (Wright 1989). The move toward the provision of full-time degree courses in abstract knowledge and literary presentation for those of a particular age group and narrow social background is part of what has been termed 'academic drift' (Pratt and Burgess 1974). While this term helps to encapsulate the process by which alternatives are transformed into conventional patterns and values, it misses the oppositional element that exists in higher education.

The tradition of more open access and part-time education is embodied in a range of institutions: the Workers' Educational Association, Birkbeck College, Ruskin College, local authority colleges and the extra-mural departments. Indeed, many practitioners refer to these roots when discussing their own efforts to mount and maintain this type of provision. There is a large and expanding area of work, loosely described as continuing education, which can run either in tandem, separately or within conventional programmes. Despite the concerns of some commentators (Pratt and Burgess 1974) that the public sector is being 'conventionalized', we maintain that there has been a parallel, if unplanned, increase in provision for mature and employed students. The Department of Education and Science acknowledged in 1986 that the numbers of part-time students had doubled since 1970 with most of that increase taking place during the 1970s (Department of Education and Science 1986b). This arose largely from unplanned local initiatives undertaken for a mixture of educational and social reasons outside the main framework of educational planning.

Higher education and Neo-Liberalism

The oil crisis in 1974, resulting in increases in inflation and unemployment, provided the impetus for a review of the aims and practices of the social democratic framework. The Great Debate initiated by the Callaghan government in 1976 encouraged a public discussion about the defects of the system of education in England and Wales. Dissatisfaction, especially with the alleged lack of fit between education and the economy, began to be voiced by opinion makers and client groups (Salter and Tapper 1981). To economists like Bacon and Eltis (1976) the welfare state appeared as a voracious leviathan consuming national wealth. State services were seen as inefficient and ineffectual forms of social engineering. Education was singled out as a high consumer taking resources away from the wealth creating private sector.

The rise of what has variously been termed Neo-Liberalism, the New Right or Thatcherism provides the new political economy framework within which policies, changes and assessments of higher education are conducted (Bosanquet 1983; Gamble 1988). Changes to the organization and operation, as well as the purposes, of higher education are taking place in terms of the goals of economy, efficiency and effectiveness. The challenge to higher education is but one aspect of a questioning of the role of all public institutions in terms of the assumed negative economic effects of public expenditure. The curtailment of incremental budgeting (where submitted budgets were automatically adjusted annually) had led by 1981 to a real reduction in recurrent expenditure on higher education.

It is possible to detect three interconnected strands in the application of market principles to higher education in the last decade. All three are underpinned by strong economic and financial considerations, based on the neo-liberal perspective, and giving rise to the accusation that educational policy has been subsumed under economic policy.

Consumer orientation

A greater stress has been placed on the consumer, giving rise to the demand for more consumer accountability and client control. This has extended the power of individual and corporate stake holders in the activities of higher education and has led to the criticism of welfare state professionals that they are over-bureaucratic, unresponsive to client needs, self-regarding and for the most part accountable only to their professional groupings. What has been termed 'producer capture' has been a focus of criticism from the political left as well as the right, who maintain that only market forces will produce effective consumer accountability. It is certainly the case that academics have possessed a high degree of self-regulation and that as far as responsiveness and accountability are concerned they are open to similar criticisms to those levelled at welfare professionals (Wilding 1987; Heald 1983). The University Grants Committee, for example, was seen as a 'dons' cartel' with planning based on the 'private college' of academic subjects controlled by 'subject barons' (Trow 1989).

Changes in financing have been proposed which are intended to make institutions more competitive, shifting the emphasis away from supplier led education to a system where the providers are more responsive to the requirements of consumers. To achieve this a series of measures aimed at enhancing the purchasing power of the individual consumer have been accompanied by moves to reduce state dependence through encouraging institutions to seek more of their funding from outside sources. One such measure is contract funding, where the funding body simply acts as a purchaser of services. The intention is to instil an element of inter-institutional competition which will supposedly enhance cost consciousness and in turn could stimulate new techniques and new markets. A customer orientation requires managers to evaluate the quality of the product and modify it in respect of changes in demand. We will return to the detailed analysis of some of the implications of financial changes for part-time provision in Chapter 4.

The demand for accountability

There has been a demand for forms of accountability more in line with those operated in commercial organizations where input/output models typically act as the basis for evaluating performance. Thus, value for money has become a high priority on the higher education agenda. A managerialist approach demands the clarification of objectives and the consideration of different and more effective forms of management. One weakness of incremental budgeting has been its in-built tendency to inhibit a rethink of priorities and methods of achieving objectives. A sequence of reports shows the government taking a much more direct interest in the tightening of economic and managerial control. There has also been a demand for adequate performance indicators. Performance indicators provide organizational information and market intelligence intended to assist institutional responsiveness to changing circumstances. They are also concerned with the quality of the product, including the appraisal of teaching, learning and research. This more rational approach to the operation of higher education does mean that institutional goals have to be set and aims and objectives clarified at every level of academic organization.

Established methods of planning and organization have come under scrutiny. In the university sector the Jarratt Report addressed the problem of efficiency, advocating strategic planning and a corporate approach combining academic, financial and managerial objectives (Jarratt 1985). It also questioned the structure and role of the University Grants Committee. The Croham Committee recommended a unified system of planning for higher education with a United Kingdom commission integrating all levels of transbinary provision (Croham 1987). Both these reports and the 1987 White Paper advocated the use of performance indicators as a managerial tool to overhaul and rationalize the system. Questions were raised about the control of academic standards in the universities and a number of subject reviews were carried out (Edward 1988; Stone 1988). One of the last acts of the University Grants Committee was to initiate reviews of university cost centres in order to establish research gradings which in turn would affect future funding.

The more collegiate approach to management in the universities contrasts with the polytechnics which, from their inception, have had a more corporate and top-down management structure. While the universities protected their unit of resource – the amount of money per student – the polytechnics reduced their unit by enrolling more students for little or no additional funds. Since the cost of a university student is on average £5,276 a year, compared to £3,325 in a polytechnic, politicians and the polytechnics' own directors have held them up as being cost efficient and more responsive to demand (Hansard 10 February 1989). This has led to some reconsideration of the substance of the differences between the sectors and to a certain competitive antagonism.

In what was the public sector of higher education there had been a partnership between local authorities, the National Advisory Body (NAB), the Council for National Academic Awards (CNAA) and the providing institutions which offered a forum for the discussion of financial, academic and social accountability. Many local authorities had policies for continuing education based on an ethos of public service and low fees which linked school, further and higher education and which frequently encouraged part-time provision. The CNAA for its part moved further towards extending access to non-standard entrants and waiving 'A' level requirements. Similarly, the NAB under Sir Christopher Ball encouraged the extension of part-time provision. However, the polytechnics and many colleges have recently acquired self-validating status and so freedom from the CNAA. They have also gained corporate status thus breaking the link with local authority control. In the meantime the NAB has been replaced by the Polytechnic and Colleges Funding Council (PCFC).

Higher education and economic policy

One consistent theme of government policy has been the emphasis on the importance of education to the post-industrial economy and Britain's international competitiveness. This echoes concerns dating from the late nineteenth century (Barnett 1986; Weiner 1981) and has led to engineering and science being designated as 'favoured areas'. In the polytechnics there has been an increase in funding for them in contrast to social science and humanities and financial protection in cases of falling student demand.

There have been a series of initiatives attempting to produce a better fit between education and the requirements of industry and commerce. The central initiative for many of these programmes has not been Department of Education and Science but the Department of Trade and Industry, acting through a quango – the Manpower Services Commission (MSC). The MSC has targeted most of its programmes to date on secondary and further education. The significance for continuing education is that it indicates a view of education as something broader than the activities encapsulated in schooling and that there are stake holders other than educators involved. The Technical and Vocational Education Initiative (TVEI) and the Schools–Industry Liaison Officer network provided a variety of support, educational experiences and agents to promote change. Science and practical subjects were encouraged with an emphasis on knowing how (technique) as opposed to the usual knowing that (knowledge). In reality the distinction is blurred; but the shift indicates a parallel change in attitude towards the purpose of schooling and as such has been subject to political and educational criticisms over the issues of selection, control and the purposes of education (Edgley 1978; Dale 1985).

The school system, with its revised content and methods and its new emphasis upon skills attainment rather than mere knowledge, is producing students who do not fit the conventional expectations of higher education. Such students may be less prepared to accept higher education unless it provides them with skills which they believe are worth having. Higher education must learn to attract them both at 18+ and as mature students already practising professional skills. This change from below has been acknowledged (Committee of Vice Chancellors and Principals 1986), yet it remains the case that large numbers of young people are leaving school with vocational qualifications rather than 'A' levels; they will only be attracted to courses which meet their need for appropriate transferable skills.

The emphasis on the provision of skills which are transferable to the world of employment is exemplified by the Council for Industry and Higher Education, which has warned of a need for an education better suited to the demands of the post-industrial society. It advocates a broader general education and pedagogy which builds upon experience as opposed to prior knowledge in the development of appropriate transferable skills (Council for Industry and Higher Education 1987). The government, through the Training Agency, has promoted the Enterprise in Higher Education Initiative in which funds were made available to institutions who were prepared to insert enterprise into the curriculum. This incentive also stimulated a review of methods and the aims and objectives of current practices. It could lead to a more flexible and heterogeneous approach, opening the way to the provision of part-time programmes for a more diverse audience (Educational Development Group 1990).

This piecemeal process of restructuring higher education towards a more market-oriented, utilitarian approach was consolidated in the Education Reform Act of 1988. The Act created the University Funding Council (UFC) and the Polytechnic and Colleges Funding Council (PCFC), granting corporate status to many institutions within the latter. The personnel and administrative structure of these bodies reflected a move away from the representation of academic interests towards those of business, administrators and financial managers. In the PCFC sector this has been paralleled in the new administrative structures and the composition of their governing bodies. A market element of contract funding was introduced to encourage competition and efficiency. The Act enhanced central control and the powers of the Secretary of State thus reducing considerably the space for professional educators to determine the direction of provision and educational policy within a broad framework of government policy (Editorial, *Times Higher Educational Supplement* 1988).

Unresolved issues

A number of inherent contradictions underpin the new framework for higher education policy. At the structural level there is a centralizing and bureaucratic tendency. Yet one of the objectives was to free institutions, making them the locus of reorganization and strategic planning. Planning is supposed to be local and institutional rather than national; managerially, it will be top down. Yet even with limited contract funding and the raising of external finance, the funding councils will remain the major purchasers and will make comparative judgements on quantity and quality. So while Sir Ron Dearing claims that the Polytechnic and Colleges Funding Council is not a planning body, it operates in ways similar to those of its predecessor, the National Advisory Body, though without any apparent grand design. Moreover, funding methodologies are not neutral techniques but reflect policy, which in turn contains priorities and educational objectives. Financial frameworks structure educational possibilities. The government's own position is ambivalent. Redefining its role from that of the guardian of the public funded system to just another customer belies its financial and political power to achieve its own objectives. These government objectives have been attacked by some educationalists (Warnock 1989; Johnson 1989) as mere political dogma.

In a market the consumer is meant to be sovereign. The insertion of market characteristics into the higher education system still begs questions. Who is the client? Who are the different stake holders? How are their different needs and purchasing capacities to be represented in the system? Different stake holders have different performance expectations. Here tensions emerge between managerialists and consumerists. As Kogan (1986) states: 'Consumerists' critiques of professional power might lead to demands for using more rather than less resources and for more concern about the immediacy of impact than about whether an input produces an effective output.'

Those in higher education are now being asked to justify its value and practices in the production and dissemination of knowledge. Questions concerning who should be educated, for how long and in what types of knowledge and methods, have moved towards the centre of the politics of education debate. A fundamental difference between the present political economy of higher education and its social democratic predecessor is over the emphasis placed on problems of demand for education and the distribution and level of consumption. The social democratic approach saw education as unequally distributed and as providing both private and social benefits – or externalities. The notion of educational opportunity meant that the state engineered chances for under-consumers, linking the desire for equitable treatment with utilitarian concerns for social gain. Given equal opportunities, an individual's capacities would be developed and rewarded meritocratically. Stress was placed on the input of people and resources not outcomes. More resources equalled better education which in turn produced economic growth. The neo-liberals reject the significance of externalities, addressing the negative effects of public expenditure. They see higher education as a benefit accruing chiefly to the individual consumer. Hence the arguments that higher education is better distributed through market mechanisms and that those who benefit should bear more of the cost. The emphasis in higher education policy shifted from managing consumption through increasing inputs of resources to an attempt to reduce public funding and relate it to specific outcomes. Generally, in education this requires us to ask what we are getting for our money.

Accepted educational practices are now being challenged by the criterion of efficiency. This requires educators to clarify the relationship between content and usage. It should encourage a greater responsiveness to students' needs and allow for an assessment of quality in terms of what is being developed in the student rather than what qualifications the student has on entry. While market forces can lead to such issues being raised, we will require performance indicators constructed with an educational sensitivity based not on cheapness masquerading as economic efficiency but on a set of educational and social objectives (Barnett 1988).

These possibilities must be viewed in the context of a system of finance that is overwhelmingly dependent on the state and its distributing agents, the UFC and PCFC. In terms of overall growth, patterns of provision and the widening of access, much will depend upon the market strength of each institution and the 'price' of different types of student. Well established institutions may prefer to maintain their market share of 'higher priced' types of students with little or no expansion of student places. In the case of part-time provision, the government, encouraged by increased numbers, is prepared to do very little in terms of support. We question the longer-term wisdom of this in Chapter 4, arguing that encouragement of part-time higher education might, in cost benefit terms, be highly efficient and make an essential contribution to a range of policy objectives.

Nevertheless, there is some evidence of a desire to address the issue of wider access. Mature students are now considered in future planning (Department of Education and Science 1988b) and the proportion in the system is beginning to rise. The collection of more precise data by the state and the institutions on a greater variety of student types provides evidence for a more heterogeneous demand. Both funding councils have now acknowledged the importance of part-time students, with the PCFC making them a distinct category in the bidding process (Universities Funding Council 1989; Polytechnic and Colleges Funding Council 1989b). At the same time the infusion of market principles into the system has led institutional managements to seek new patterns of demand.

However, the proposed treatment of 'less advantaged groups' is paradoxical. The Department of Education and Science notes that 'mature students may not be willing to accept a drop in income (or potential income) for the duration of the course' (Department of Education and Science 1986a, p. 4). The more recent White Paper on student support (Department of Education and Science 1988c) recommends top-up loans: a form of finance most disadvantageous to these very mature students. Once again we can contrast the aim of increasing access with a funding policy which at best does nothing for part-time students or full-time mature students, particularly those from lower socio-economic groups. Indeed, concern has been expressed about the likely deterrent effect on adult returners of proposed fee changes (Smith and Saunders 1989b; National Institute of Adult and Continuing Education 1989). To the extent that the government does take access seriously it does so in terms of its rewriting of the Robbins' principle, which becomes 'Courses of higher education should be available for all those who are qualified by ability and attainment to pursue them . . . but . . . the benefit has to be sufficient to justify the cost' (Department of Education and Science 1985b). What really constitutes benefit according to some recent interpretations is that which serves the needs of the economy (O'Leary 1987). So access is important not because of a commitment to ideals of education or civilized humanity but because the economy requires more graduates and higher education must be more responsive in their production.

The pressure for reform and expansion

The developing policy and planning framework is being confronted by three pressures. One is political: the publicly stated desire for expansion. The second is change in the demographic structure. These together have an effect on a third factor: that of changes in the amount and type of manpower required by a technologically based economy.

Expansion and government policy

In early 1989 Kenneth Baker called for a large increase in participation rates to 20 per cent by 1995 and 30 per cent by 2000 (Baker 1989a). However, it is wise to clarify the terms used when looking at future projections. The age participation index (API) refers to 18-year-olds or 'young persons'. This group is quite distinctive, forming the basis of most planning and taking the lion's share of resources. A 'participation rate', like Mr Baker's 30 per cent or his doubling of student participation (though not numbers) is a blanket term. It could mean nearly a third of the population, a cohort over a generation or, more probably, raw numbers. The statement was taken as an aspiration to widen access to higher education rather than as a serious projection of numbers. A more precise figure was provided by junior minister Robert Jackson, who predicted over one million students in 1990. The present Secretary of State, John MacGregor, is less bullish than his predecessor, reverting to the API and targeting around 23 per cent participation by the end of the century. Whatever the true figure, all of these predictions commit higher education to increasing access and assume that increasing access also means widening access. It is always wise to read claims for expansion with some scepticism: after all, Mrs Thatcher in 1972 promised a participation rate of 22 per cent by 1981. Demographic factors and current school practices mean that expansion on the scale proposed is unlikely to be achieved without a substantial influx of those labelled 'continuing education students'. Indeed the White Paper on student loans relies heavily on an increase in mature students, especially women, ethnic minorities and what are euphemistically referred to as 'less advantaged social groups'. Part-time provision must play some part in any subsequent growth.

What is apparent is that the government, in line with its public expenditure policy, is not prepared to provide additional funding. In the House of Commons debate on student loans the Secretary of State stated that while he wished to see student numbers reaching two million by 2015, higher education could not 'realistically expect to win an significantly greater share of public money than it already had'. Therefore expansion must come from efficient management and rationalization coupled with external sources of income. Resource issues also raise serious questions about the quality of education. To those like Robert Jackson who appear to believe that the unit of resource is being used as a tactic to preserve privilege, the concerns expressed by educators coping with increasing numbers fall on deaf ears. In the 1960s it was demonstrated that more need not mean worse; but the expansion that took place then was supported by investment and some thought had been given to how greater numbers would be integrated. No such conditions hold today and anxieties are being voiced by educators, especially within the PCFC sector, where unit costs have already been reduced by 20 per cent in the last decade. To say that more will mean different does not solve the quality problem voiced by individual consumers and employers alike. Politicians talk about excellence yet hope that market forces will hold or drive up standards. Expansion and excellence are not mutually exclusive; but quality control could cost money.

Demographic trends and the impetus to reform

Changes in age structure, socio-economic groupings, sex ratios and ethnic distribution do not in themselves determine specific education policies. The significance and treatment of such factors comes from their political standing in the policy process, presenting a range of possible courses of action. However, such changes do demand a policy response since they can require changes to current expenditure programmes and have an impact on our social and economic institutions. Undoubtedly, the sudden interest in continuing education, and particularly its part-time form, has been prompted by public recognition of demographic changes of a dramatic kind. The government has based its policies on the number of 16–19-year-olds available at given dates to enter employment or further education. Projections showed a decline in this age group of nearly a quarter between 1987 and 1996. It was assumed that this decline would be paralleled in the numbers entering higher education. The so-called demographic time bomb projects a reduction in the number of 18-year-olds from one million plus in 1982 to under 660,000 in 1995 (Statistical Report *Training Skills Bulletin* 1988). Hence the encouragement to widen access and increase the participation rate of that cohort.

A more considered look at population projections has allayed some of the worst fears of the consequences for higher education of a declining market. The Institute of Manpower Studies at Sussex University has pointed to a disparity in the figures between different socio-economic groups (Pearson and Pike 1989a). While acknowledging an overall decline in the 18+ cohort they point out that this decline is greater in lower socio-economic groups, whereas higher education recruits disproportionately from groups I and II. For example, these groups comprised 32 per cent of the population in 1987, yet accounted for 60 per cent of the university population. What is more, the dramatic fall in 18-year-olds from socio-economic groups 111-V (reaching 50 per cent by 1995) must be weighed against the relative decline of these groups in the socio-economic structure. There has been a growth of skilled occupations and a decline in manual and semiskilled occupations so we would expect an increase in upward mobility and a subsequent expansion of categories I and II. There is also a growing recognition of the contribution of parental education to the level of take up rates for higher education. Burnhill *et al.* (1989) suggest that any post-compulsory education undertaken by parents, whatever its level, boosts the likelihood of their children qualifying for higher education. While the Department of Education and Science has previously acknowledged the possibility of parental influence it assumed that only graduate status was significant.

The government now explains the recent expansion of demand for higher education in terms of improved schooling. It argues that, as a result of government policy, more qualifications are being gained by a smaller cohort. There is certainly some truth in this, though the expansion has not been so much in 'A' level results as in other qualifications. 'A' levels have remained at what a Department of Education and Science official has described as 'an inevitable plateau' (Sofer 1988), at around 14 per cent of the population for the last decade. Alternatives to 'A' levels could produce a substantial demand for degree level work if barriers to access were to be removed. However, for the moment, 'A' level standard entrance remains the predominant mode of selection. Greater numbers of school students, especially girls, have gained minimum entry requirements; but this has been in part a result of greater numbers in the age group.

The gloomy prognostications for the mid-1990s, when the decline in the major participating group will be at its lowest, are undergoing optimistic modifications. The application and admission figures of the University Central Council for Admissions (UCCA) and the Polytechnic Central Admissions Service (PCAS) have reached an all-time high. Universities in 1988–89 showed an increase of 9.7 per cent over their 1987–88 figures in applications from home-based candidates (Universities Central Council for Admissions 1988). Figures for the polytechnics and colleges of higher education are not amenable to direct comparison because in 1989 they also handled applications for other qualifications. However, it has been estimated (Segal 1989) that their applications are up by about 3 per cent over the previous year's figures. This student boom is set to continue in 1990 with an increase in applications. Smithers and Robinson (1989) therefore conclude that fears of a downturn are unfounded. On the other hand the Institute of Manpower Studies warns of a possible fall in demand resulting from the introduction of student loans, and from the competition for members of the target age group by employers offering higher wages which reflect the scarcity factor (Pearson and Pike 1989b). They are therefore less optimistic about sustaining the boom into the 1990s. One consequence may be an increase in demand for part-time provision from those working their way through college and those delaying entry as a result of financial considerations.

Another jolt to complacency occurs when we look at the distribution of demand between subjects and institutions. Despite a government policy of creating more places in physical sciences and engineering there is no evidence of unmet demand in these areas. Indeed, there has been a decline in the applications for courses in engineering over a number of years (*Times Higher Educational Supplement* 1989). Previous DES projections have also failed to take account of demand from sectors other than the 18+ cohort. Increased applications from mature students, and particularly from women, are becoming significant. In the case of mature students this has had most impact in the polytechnics and colleges. There has been an increase in the proportion of women in full-time higher education across the board (Department of Education and Science 1988b).

The potential demand by minority ethnic groups and older persons may also have been underestimated. Most ethnic minority families have lower age profiles, so the proportion of those aged 18+ will rise in the 1990s. While the majority come from socio-economic groups III-V, there is a growing encouragement from families to obtain mobility and professional status through education. Sadly, this is not always reinforced by the schools, so continuing education is a focus for those who wish to 'get on' but are relatively unqualified. The changing age structure will produce increasing numbers of active persons over the formal retirement age who may wish to seek higher education. One in six people in England is over 65-year-old and by 2020 the figure will be one in four. Moreover, there are those in middle age who wish to change their occupation and restructure their lives in preparation for a fulfilling retirement. Others may take or be forced into early retirement. The neglect of these various categories of the ageing has a strong cultural basis, though the rationale appears to be that they are not seen to be worth the investment in education and retraining. Peter Laslett (1989) has detailed the potential economic and social contribution of those who have completed their productive lives and entered the 'third age'. Continuing education could make a strong case, economically as well as socially, for the inclusion of older age groups in educational planning and provision. At the most pragmatic level they could assist in filling skill shortages.

Manpower requirements

Currently there is a substantial graduate shortfall. The Institute of Manpower Studies estimates that demand for graduates will have increased by 30 per cent by the year 2000 by which time there will have been a 25 per cent decline in the number of 18-year-olds (Pearson and Pike 1989b). A recent survey of 153 major companies reports that 83 per cent of them were trying to take measures to overcome graduate shortages in the 1990s (PA Consulting Group 1989). These include sponsoring students, accepting less well qualified candidates for posts, looking more favourably at mature candidates and trying to entice women graduates back into work. These companies are particularly concerned about the lack of graduate engineers, computer specialists and technologists where the failure to substantially increase graduates is compounded by the higher than average 14 per cent drop out rate in the universities among those with lower 'A' level grades (Institute of Manpower Studies 1988).

Industry complains of the inappropriateness of much education to its needs. John Banham has stated bluntly that 'Education is too important to be left in the hands of educationalists, business must enter the secret garden' (Banham 1987). A study by Boys *et al.* (1989) suggests that industry may not fully understand or express its own needs. While employers claim to want graduates with personal, social and communication skills, they actually seek science and engineering graduates whose courses, they suggest, provide highly specific and less transferable skills. Boys *et al.* also claim to observe different values on the part of students, with humanities students less interested in the rewards of salary, promotion and fringe benefits in contrast to opportunities for creativity, originality and variety of experience. This difference, they argue, is significant in explaining the differential rates of graduate unemployment acknowledged in earlier studies (Brennan and McGeevor 1985). Humanities students take longer to find suitable employment because they are more choosy. However, there is no major long-term problem in finding employment for graduates irrespective of discipline and with an estimated 7 per cent increase in demand for graduates this situation is likely to continue (Central Service Unit for Career Services in Universities and Polytechnics 1988). The increased demand has had its effect upon graduate salaries. The same body gives the median figure for graduate starting salaries in 1988 as £9,300. The PA Consulting Group (1989) survey gives an average industrial starting salary of £10,015, but a London average of £11,389. This starting salary is likely to increase by some 70 per cent after five years in the industrial and financial sectors. The real crisis is perhaps most likely to hit the public rather than the private sector. Not only are starting salaries lower in the public sector but growth is slower. Compare the 70 per cent increase in salaries within five years in industry with a mere 40 per cent in teaching.

Certainly employers could express more accurately their requirements and put more money into the system, particularly for continuing education. This is not to deny the existence of good sponsorship schemes and in-house partnerships; but many employers have little idea as to how to respond to labour supply problems. Higher education must realize that in spite of increased applications they will be competing with employers for young people in the 1990s. Continuing education could be a focal point for all their concerns.

Mature students and higher education

It is hardly surprising, given demographic predictions and graduate shortfalls, that continuing education has been seen by some as a panacea. It appeared as such on the political agenda in the White Paper of 1987. The Institute of Manpower Studies maintains that we need to increase the number of mature and vocationally qualified students by 50 per cent to meet future manpower requirements (Pearson and Pike 1989b). The growth in mature students is impressive, amounting to one in six of entrants to higher education overall. Government figures (Department of Education and Science 1988b) show a growth in first-year mature student numbers in British higher education of 42 per cent between 1979–80 and 1986–87. Of the 186,000 mature students in 1986–87, 83 per cent were at polytechnics or colleges of higher education. Two-thirds of mature students undertake subdegree level work and the figures also include postgraduate students aged over 25. Only 15 per cent of these mature students were actually studying for a first degree. Only about one-third (60,000) were studying full-time, the remaining 126,300 being part-time (Department of Education and Science 1989b).

A major concern about mature student entrants has been their relative lack of 'standard' entry requirements; that is to say, their lack of 'normal' 'A' level scores. Concerns about the academic suitability of those with non-standard or vocational qualifications have been expressed by some academics (Smithers and Robinson 1989), for whom 'A' level scores are central to the equitable allocation of scarce places. Fulton and Ellwood (1989) have pointed to the adverse effects of this admissions policy on levels of non-standard entry. Indeed the CNAA was very conscious of this criticism in developing its own policy towards non-standard entry. Evans says 'many of the uncertainties that tutors express about the initial entry of those lacking normal qualifications stem from the . . . lack of reliable evidence of achievement' (Evans 1984) and goes on to suggest ways of assessing potential. That the polytechnics and colleges of higher education have successfully done so is shown clearly by the findings of Bourner and Hamed. Their study compared the results of standard and non-standard entry students on CNAA degrees and came to the conclusion that 'On average, those with non-standard entry qualifications fared at least as well as those in the other broad categories' (Bourner and Hamed 1987a). They further noted that degree performance appears to improve with age up to the age of about 40 (Bourner and Hamed 1987b). This is important since the term mature student can mean several things; but to those in manpower and educational planning it frequently refers to those in their 20s. Indeed, the Department of Education and Science now distinguishes between the Young Mature Entry Index (comprising initial entrants aged 21–24 regardless of qualification) and the old Mature Participation Index (aged 25 and over). Both these categories are expressed as percentages of other significant populations.

We wish to argue that the debate about mature students and entry qualifications is posed the wrong way round. While concern is expressed about entry standards and their ability to predict a 'good degree', perhaps we should concern ourselves more with exit standards. Performance indicators could be devised to support institutions not on the basis of the quality of students which enter but the qualities with which they depart. This value-added notion of higher education concentrates on what can be developed for specified object-ives. In contrast the system is still mainly geared to rewarding those who, while undoubtedly intelligent, have already benefited from large inputs of good schooling. It is fairly obvious that those taking courses which assume 'A' level standard will have more chance of success if they have already achieved at that level.

It might also be possible to rethink the appropriateness of the content of higher education in terms of the market requirements of its graduates. Science and technology courses are often described as linear in that they are said to require to be taught with cumulative complexity, with students progressing through each stage in turn. While there is a genuine demand for graduates who may well have been recruited through an 'A' level route there may also be a need for a rethink about the width and relevance of some of their courses. After all, while employers may think that they need graduates who are potential Nobel Prize winners, there are many jobs in applied science, intermediate technology and engineering that require general skills rather than academic excellence. We must guard against substituting credentialism for relevant education based upon stated purposes. The alternative is what Berg (1973) has called the great training robbery where people are overqualified for their position in an advanced division of labour.

The growth and distribution of part-time provision

Only recently has there been an acknowledgement of the substantial quantity and variety of part-time routes available within higher education. Between 1975 and 1986 the total number of part-time students increased by 62 per cent compared with a rise of only 18 per cent in full-time higher education (Department of Education and Science 1988b). The most recently published official statistics are for the year 1986–87 and we have attempted to summarize them in Table 2.1. The total number of students in British higher education is given as 945,000 (including overseas students). Of these nearly 38 per cent (358,700) were part-time and over two-thirds were in polytechnics and colleges of higher education. Not all, of course, were on degree level programmes. Of particular significance is the growth of part-time numbers at subdegree level. Since the mid-1970s there has been a 60 per cent growth in subdegree work, predominantly in the polytechnics and colleges of higher education. By comparison there has been a fall of 39 per cent in full-time subdegree work, with the consequence that the part-time mode has virtually substituted for full-time provision in this area. While institutions do not always enhance their status by taking on such work – given the tendency to see status in terms of the level of academic programmes – this increase in numbers does illustrate the responsiveness of these institutions to the demands of employers and the local community. It also suggests that partnerships between the state, professional organizations, institutions and employers can operate to their mutual benefit.

At postgraduate level there has been a 75 per cent growth in part-time students during the same period (1975–76 to 1986–87) amounting to 43 per

Table 2.1 Part-time students in higher education

	Part-time numbers	Percentage of total	Sub-degree	Degree	Post-graduate	Percentage increase 1975–76– 1986–87
Polytechnics and colleges	234,500	66.5	189,400	27,100	18,000	70
Universities	44,600	12.0	3,400	6,100	35,100	58
Open University	79,600	21.5	9,300	69,300	1,000	45
Total	358,700	100	202,100	102,500	54,100	62

Sources: Social Trends (1988) and DES (1988a).

cent of all postgraduate students. The growth appears to relate to a combination of factors: the desire of many colleges to develop their postgraduate work
(and so their status); an increase in the demand for postgraduate courses and
so the number of postgraduates overall; and a shortage of research council
funds (the main source of funding for full-time postgraduate students). There
may also have been an increased preference at master's level for working and
studying at the same time, though the extent to which this is a forced choice is
not possible to determine. Nevertheless, the increase in postgraduate part-
time numbers is such that it clearly is an acceptable and effective means of
expanding the sector. The research councils might consider putting their
limited resources into funding all students' fees rather than wholly supporting
very limited numbers of full-time students.

At undergraduate level most part-time students work through the Open
University (69,300). Most of the rest (27,000) are at polytechnics and colleges
of higher education. Despite an apparently impressive 58 per cent increase in
the period 1975–76 to 1986–87 the universities still only had 6,100 part-time
degree level students registered with them at the end of this period.

Future policy developments

Continuing and part-time education are now much more to the fore of policy
agenda. As higher education becomes more politicized we need to look at
where continuing education will be located in a reordered system. If it is to
become more central, a rethink about the very nature of higher education in
this country will be required. At the moment different definitions are held by
contending groups within education. The meaning which continuing education comes to have will depend upon the outcome of a struggle to control
education. In favour of a stronger continuing education dimension are the
PCFC institutions and an increasing number of universities. The Department
of Education and Science and the government want expansion (though the
former appears uncertain as to how much it actually wants) and this has at
least meant that official statistics are now pertinent to the debate. There has
also been a growth in interest groups, like the transbinary Association for
Part-time Higher Education (APHE).

Part-time higher education undoubtedly could make an important contribution to the restructuring and expansion of higher education, but there
remain large gaps between the rhetoric of intent and practical policies to
achieve desired objectives. There are also divisions within those who would
claim to be friends of continuing education concerning its definition and its
relation to the rest of the system. As a consequence the various policy making
bodies continue to operate in a contradictory and confusing manner. Two
distinct policy perspectives can be identified which can assist us in interpreting
current trends and future prospects. We will call these the 'weathering the
storm' perspective, and the 'continuing education', perspective.

Weathering the storm

This perspective uses the age participation index (API) as the basis of planning for higher education. Demographic factors are seen as creating manpower shortages as well as underrecruitment to higher education, with the consequent threat to the survival of some departments and even institutions. Hence the encouragement of new client groups like ethnic minorities, women and mature students. This view of the need to stimulate demand extends to the Institute of Manpower Studies, which advocates an increase in the numbers staying on at school and an alteration in admission procedures to include alternative and vocational qualifications. The problem is that rarely, if at all, has any of this been thought through in educational terms. Different social factors are presented as individual variables which can contribute to an expansion of the system. Having stated the variables and their recommendations about what should be done (usually involving institutions taking more of each category) the educational and financial requirements are left unconsidered. There may be sound reasons for the low participation of some groups which will not wither away merely because there is a perceived need to increase numbers. A proper consideration of these reasons could inform us about how to encourage and sustain such students. However, too often this approach judges higher education mainly by external economic criteria, processing inputs into outputs which in their turn become useful economic inputs. What is lacking is a strategy.

This version of weathering the storm – what might be called the economistic version – at least has a rationale for extending the system, involving a recognition of the need for structural and cultural changes. A more cynical view sees continuing education as something that can be manipulated as a makeweight until demographic trends right themselves. Neither view systematically considers either the interrelation of the different patterns of demand or the variety of policy packages (extending beyond education) for supporting these students; nor do they consider the necessary adjustments to higher education which will ensue. The conventional paradigm holds, in spite of great changes to the system. The Department of Education and Science, although aware of increasing demand, still planned in the February 1989 expenditure White Paper for a fall in full-time equivalent student numbers in 1991. This was adjusted in the November statement in the light of the increase in numbers of those staying on at school after the age of 16, so that the number of full-time and sandwich course students is now set to rise by 50,000 in the period 1988–89 to 1992–93 (HMSO 1989). Provision for fee increases, which will be of up to £1,675 and will come into effect in 1990–91, has been made in respect of these additional full-time students. The switch from recurrent funding to fees is claimed to be financially neutral (MacGregor 1989a), with support for full-time, 18-year-old students to be calculated as a combination of maintenance grants, fees and top up loans (HMSO 1989). From the viewpoint of part-time students paying their own fees financial neutrality takes on a new meaning.

At worst a weathering the storm approach will bolt on to the system certain cosmetic changes which are peripheral to mainstream developments. Plans in both sectors are for expansion, with some universities and polytechnics proposing massive increases in student numbers. Yet the rate of expansion, its geographical location, as well as the type of subject and student remain problematic. Two sets of questions are left unanswered by the proponents of this approach. First, is the magnitude of growth sustainable after 1993, and how is it understood within the institutions? Is there to be an overall expansion, or merely an increase in the market share of desirable fee payers by a particular institution or sector? Second, given an expansion based upon charging fees near to full cost mainly for full-time students, how are we to deal with the social objectives of continuing education? The limited coordination between different facets of policy affects the attainment of stated objectives. There is the danger of a policy of stop go, with the consequence that demand created at one level, for example in schools or by employers, is blocked by a lag in other institutional arrangements. The reverse is also possible, where places are created in higher education for which there is insufficient demand. Most frequently problems centre on admissions procedures and the lack of part-time modes of provision. With rapid expansion doubts are raised about the quality of education as students are packed into classes. We must be wary of expansion under the current resource distribution and income maximization regime which jeopardizes part-time programmes in either quantity or quality.

Continuing education perspective

What we term the continuing education perspective views changes as opportunities to advance educational and social principles. It seeks to interpret recent developments in terms of their contribution to specified educational objectives. Unlike either version of weathering the storm this approach starts with an access policy based upon broad objectives as well as an understanding of how they might be met. Given stated objectives, a policy framework could include packages of financial and educational support targeted at different potential participants. The framework would have to recognize possible conflicts between objectives and the fact that rarely can the educational and financial needs of an individual or group be encapsulated in a single policy envelope. One obvious conflict at present is between the objective of increasing technical manpower and the objective of increasing the participation of mature students. On the whole mature students tend not to favour technological courses even though technological skills are in short supply. It becomes necessary to clarify the policy objectives. Are they predominantly educational, economic, or both? The concentration on economic objectives takes us down a more utilitarian educational path. It is quite possible to target potential students and develop a package which will fulfil such a set of objectives. The CNAA has promoted conversion courses for women into engineering and the Training Agency, with BP, is developing a degree built on the Technical and

Vocational Education Initiative (TVEI) and the Youth Training Scheme (YTS) (Claridge 1989). In comparison to Baker's mass higher education, such schemes are expensive, dependent on selective funds and limited to a minority.

The current framework sees the funding bodies distributing state funds. Their main concern appears to be the principle of financial accountability and the insertion of market principles into what is still a bureaucratic distribution. So far these bodies seem more geared to saving money than promoting education. One of the advantages of the previous funding bodies – the National Advisory Body and the University Grants Committee – was their capacity to advise government on educational needs. This meant that if any of the educational partners, particularly the providing institutions, wished to set themselves certain goals then there was a forum for discussion of the support needed to achieve them. This is not to say that they would get the support, nor is it to deny a degree of over planning of the public sector by the National Advisory Body.

It could be argued that the current financial framework is open and flexible enough to embrace an expansion of continuing education. After all market signals are sent down from the funding bodies about a range of possible developments. Similarly, signals move upwards from the institutions indicating their response. An example in the PCFC sector is the objective of wider access. Here there is an intention to increase support for part-time provision (Polytechnic and Colleges Funding Council 1989b, section 7.6) which has sent a signal to institutions to create or expand courses for part-time students. Theoretically, signals may be sent in both directions, in that the adoption of a particular tactic (part-time provision) to achieve an objective (wider access) will inform the PCFC of the need to modify or abandon the objective, or at least the method of achieving it. In a similar vein the signals coming from the previous funding bodies at the times of cuts resulted in the polytechnics expanding (access) and the universities preserving the unit of resource (retrenchment).

Conclusions

An expansion of higher education in the United Kingdom to the level of the leading advanced nations will require a big change in the attitudes of the general population and within the providing institutions. Any government serious about widening access and developing education throughout life will have to give a policy lead as well as the necessary resources. A limitation of the present planning arrangements is that they are geared more to accountancy than to social and educational policies. This is not to say that an alternative approach would not be concerned with financial efficiency nor that the current approach will not yield some benefits. Planning and social policy have become pejorative terms under neo-liberal politics. Nevertheless targeting and financing those sections of the society which in the main are non-participants, and providing a variety of courses, some of which will be directly related to manpower needs, do involve certain aspects of the maligned social planning process. The salient feature is that of coherence: for example, the closer relationship of schooling and further education with the higher education system. This will require institutions to become more open and accountable. Without large inputs of public or private finance the distribution of resources between sectors and programmes will have to be altered. Those with privileges rarely give them up without a struggle.

There needs to be coherence not just within education but also between government departments. There is, for example, little coherence between the social security system and student support. Such coherence as there is will disappear when students are taken out of welfare. Even the proposed tripling of discretionary hardship funds for full-time students will do nothing for mature, low income part-time students or for the young on access courses. Coherence requires a recognition of the conflicting objectives of different departments of government. Nowhere is this more apparent than in the example of those wishing to attend access courses yet dependent on social security. The objective of the Department of Social Security in applying the 21-hour rule (the maximum number of hours allowed for study while also being available for work when claiming unemployment benefit) is to get people off the unemployed register. Those providing courses tend to see the issue as one of educational rights and affirmative action towards members of less privileged groups. In fact, educational opportunity is idiosyncratic in this area, dependent upon local and even individual decisions. These decisions by Department of Social Security officials even extend to whether or not a course is considered to be preparing a student for work. Educational packages must be understood in terms of the patterns of work, leisure, domestic arrangements and income. Continuing education involves more than just the intellectual life of the individual. Many of the very students that so many official reports maintain it is essential to promote are reliant for their educational experiences upon some sort of social support. Some students behave illegally in order to study. What is required is a stated educational objective and a standardized set of support procedures operating throughout the country, if we wish to move beyond the stage of posturing. Similarly, the effects of taking students out of the welfare system must be properly thought through.

In the next chapter we draw attention to some of the distinctive features of part-time degree level provision and its role in continuing education. This is based upon our research on the supply side of provision. To a considerable extent supply has created demand in higher education. In the future we will need to develop a better understanding of the life chances of potential participants and build them into policy objectives if we are serious about continuing education. This will involve a variety of packages composed of linked educational and financial items. There comes a point when in order to achieve the objectives of more participation and the preservation and enhancement of quality more resources are required. The pursuit of the objectives of privatization and deregulation (Heald 1983; Le Grand and Robinson 1984) have produced a short-term view which compounds structural problems in the economy. Under the present political economy regime it is unlikely that the necessary resources could be made available even if the government so wished. This is coupled with a negative view of public services and a rejection of the positive social functions of a welfare state in the development of the economy.

Rationalization and efficiency drives can only go so far. Further improvements in efficiency may require additional investment. For example, new methods of self-directed learning require expenditure on capital equipment and upon retraining. It is unlikely that higher education will attract a substantial influx of either public or private funds. Developments will have to take place within the kind of funding levels which currently exist. While there is no reason in principle why those monies should not be redistributed in terms of a new set of priorities, such as continuing or part-time education, we must recognize that any attempt at change will encounter the opposition a powerful status quo. To place continuing and part-time higher education nearer to the centre of the stage will require a considerable cultural shift inside academe and in the society at large. The drive for reform must be one in which the proponents of continuing and part-time education are consulted about the route and not merely included as passengers.

3 | The Structure of Part-time Degree Provision

Part-time higher education has only recently come to the fore of the political agenda, in response to wider issues of finance, expansion and control as well as demographic changes. Many universities and polytechnics have reorganized and extended their continuing education provision. Part-time provision has featured in this. However, the major developments in part-time higher education predate proposals to reorganize the system. What is more, they arose not so much from issues of national policy but rather in spite of them. As we noted in the last chapter, the post-Robbins assumptions about ability and the availability of courses helped to structure the debate about opportunity in post-school provision. Although the expansion of the 'public sector' did much to open up higher education to a wider audience and provide an alternative to the values of the universities, the sector has tended to develop as a modified extension of the principles of the meritocratic university. However, within what we characterize below as the conventional framework a number of institutions have offered a more flexible response to student demand. There has been a greater emphasis upon vocational orientation, 'useful knowledge', and sandwich provision.

A variety of interest groups, drawn from education, commerce and industry, as well as from the clients, are beginning to put forward different conceptions of the value and purposes of higher education (see Chapter 2). The business lobby is particularly interesting. Its manpower demands and conceptions of contract, efficiency and productivity are inserting elements of the ethos of privatization into higher education. The great 'noise' about the relationship between education and the economy which was supposed to develop out of the Labour Party's Great Debate of 1976 is now developing in practice, with some sections of industry attacking the failure of education to deliver the goods. Thus Banham's (1987) demand that business enter the secret garden. The granting of corporate status for the polytechnics and the predominance of business people on their boards is evidence that this is beginning to happen. The *National Association of Teachers in Further and Higher Education Journal* (NATFHE 1989), analysing the appointments of independent governors to the boards of the new corporations, found that 47.8 per cent of them were company directors, 22.3 per cent professional people and 12.7 per cent were from the public sector. Only 13 people appeared to have any connection with education. Whether business people, with their very particular interests, will cope with the needs of such complex public institutions is a matter for conjecture. This development has, however, led business to join other stake holders and practitioners in challenging conventional notions of higher education.

In this chapter and the next we will concentrate upon part-time first degree level provision. In the previous chapter first degree provision was located in the wider context of part-time higher education. While not the largest part of that provision it is a particularly significant area of part-time provision, offering as it does an alternative route to the three-year full-time model which has dominated educational thinking.

It may be useful at this point to distinguish two models which caricature the predominant features of the system: the conventional and continuing education models (Table 3.1). Both models offer legitimate and workable ways of

Table 3.1   Models of two types of higher education

	Conventional	*Continuing*
Availability	Restricted	Open
	18+	All ages
	Location specific	Multi-based network communication
	Full-time/three or four academic years	Part-time/flexitime
Activity	Specialized academic courses/socialization into academic norms	Learning tailored to a variety of needs
	Objectives assumed and taken for granted	Objectives debated and changing
	Authority vested in academics	Authority negotiated
	Students as receivers of knowledge	Clients are active in learning process
Audience	Relatively homogeneous with similar needs	Relatively heterogeneous/needs vary
	Narrow social background	Wide social composition
Evaluation	Limited to financial accounting/little emphasis on effectiveness and efficiency	Learning planned and constructed in terms of measurement and monitoring
	Quality equated with exclusion	Quality equated with both accepted standards and value-added

organizing higher education, yet, so dominant is conventional thinking that continuing education may appear to be composed of residual categories and is often perceived negatively as all those things 'normal' education is not. Part-time provision is included in continuing education in so far as its audience differs from the full-time students who have acted as the basis for planning. However, we should not assume that either part-time provision or continuing education provision are necessarily radical in all respects. There is both a strong and a weak version. The weak version increases availability (opens up access) to a slightly different audience (older) without questioning other aspects of the conventional system. For example, a part-time route to a single honours degree could be offered to older students with 'A' level entry. The strong version may be truly radical, challenging the conventional position in terms of authority, control and knowledge. As we shall see in Chapter 5, support for continuing education may mean the widening of the system or it may mean merely more of the same.

A rising chorus of concern is challenging the conventional notion of a three-year continuous, residential, honours degree, taken in a single institution, the provision of which is planned on the basis of an assumed demand of formally qualified 18–19-year-olds who wish or can be persuaded to enter. This challenge, though not confined to business, is rooted more in practical issues than the concern for equalitarian principles. As such it differs significantly from the motives of many of the pioneers of part-time provision within education. It may well also go beyond their critique of post-Robbins education, even making problematic our understanding of the term 'higher education' as well as the meaning and status of academic credentials, established forms of pedagogy and the knowledge components of the curriculum.

What is regrettable is not that such fundamental issues should be raised. Robinson has argued that these were precisely the issues that Robbins *should* have raised (Robinson 1988). It is rather that fundamental issues are raised in the context of such ignorance. At the time that our research first began the official statistics were presented in such a way that it was difficult to decipher the different modes and levels of study and to tell how many part-time students were doing first degrees. Indeed, the government approach as evinced in the planning documentation was based upon a view of the mature student and the part-time student as homogeneous categories (Department of Education and Science 1986b; Department of Education and Science 1986a). While Department of Education and Science statistics are now beginning to reflect more subtlety what is required is a specific and objective understanding of the intentions, circumstances and capacities of the mature, and of the less formally qualified, student. This in turn has to be integrated with a considered analysis of the existing provision, be it full-or part-time. Only then can we properly assess the form and content of provision appropriate for the next decade. The recent growth in part-time provision has not benefited from much systematic analysis.

Tight (1986) has mapped the geographical availability of part-time first degree level provision. Others have studied the impact of non-standard entry upon performance (Bourner and Hamed 1987a; Evans 1984). Some studies of individual degree programmes are beginning to emerge (Johnson and Hall 1985; Gallacher, Leahy and Sharp 1986). More recently an attempt has been made to describe part-time first degree level provision in Scotland (Gallacher *et al.* 1989), which will be followed by the results of the Scottish Council for Research in Education (SCRE)'s analysis of demand in the same country. In this chapter we offer a framework of national part-time first degree provision complementary to that of Tight (1986) and provide base lines of information against which effectiveness of provision may be measured. The statistical observations presented derive from our national survey. These figures are based on the academic year 1985–86, when the survey was conducted, and are restricted to degree level courses only. The numbers undertaking part-time first degrees since that time have increased. However, the research findings remain relevant. The models of provision outlined still apply and this is reflected in the nature and quality of the provision. Where recent trends are leading to changes these are indicated in the text.

Type and size of degree course

The most recent statistics on part-time degree level students were presented in Chapter 2. They indicate that the majority of part-time first degree students study with the Open University. Of the rest, less than one-fifth are at universities, and most of these are located either in London or Northern Ireland. Of the 52 university degrees which were identified by us as available to evening only students most came from a single institution – Birkbeck College. Outside London only 30 per cent of university part-time degrees were for evening students. The then 'public sector' provision both inside and outside London was and continues to be much more extensive, and is supplemented by a large number of access courses catering for those requiring pre-degree level study.

Potential students' choice of degree is even more restricted than is implied in the figures above. These refer to named degrees as they appear in institutional prospectuses. However, there is a disparity between named degrees and actual degree programmes. The 323 named degrees about which we received responses to our questionnaire in fact represented only 235 degree programmes. The difference is made up of minor variations of different combinations within each degree structure. While such variations represent genuine choices for students they also have the effect of exaggerating the apparent range and diversity of provision.

Degree courses also vary markedly by size of the student body. If potential students value the support of others in a similar position, their choice is restricted even further. As Table 3.2 shows, some degree programmes had very small numbers indeed. What is more, the size of programmes varies by sector of provision. The mean number of part-time students per university degree programme was half that of polytechnic degrees. The difference was even more

Table 3.2   Mean number of part-time students on degree by mode of attendance

	Daytime	Evening	Day and evening	All	N =
Universities					56
Mean	11.4	73.3	65.0	35.2	
Standard deviation	13.5	28.4	130.1	64.9	
Polytechnics					119
Mean	52.5	90.6	69.5	62.8	
Standard deviation	51.1	58.3	49.1	54.0	
Colleges of higher education					37
Mean	61.0	49.3	21.0	55.1	
Standard deviation	64.9	43.5	12.7	57.1	
Scottish public sector					7
Mean	66.3	68.5	–	67.6	
Standard deviation	21.4	47.4	–	35.7	
All institutions					219
Mean	44.3	75.4	64.8	54.6	
Standard deviation	50.6	50.2	84.9	57.9	

pronounced where daytime only degrees were concerned. The mean total of students on a univeristy daytime degree was 11.4 compared with 52.5 for the equivalent polytechnic course. Colleges of higher education had an even higher number of students on daytime degrees, with a mean of 61.0. The standard deviation was much greater for the 'public sector' institutions, but then each sector had some degrees with hardly any students on them. The small number of students per degree in the university sector is particularly marked. Even on evening only degrees the average number of students on university degrees was somewhat smaller than polytechnics, probably due to different levels of funding (Chapter 4), but much larger than that of the colleges of higher education.

The differences by sector are even more pronounced if we look at first year intakes only (Table 3.3). A student deciding to take a daytime only university degree would typically be one of seven part-time students in that year group. We conclude from this that many part-time students in universities are integrated into full-time degree programmes, whereas in a typical polytechnic or college of higher education degree, first year student numbers are high enough either to run separate degrees or separate part-time support units within them. Of course, some part-time students will greatly enjoy being a minority in a full-time student culture, though others will not. Certainly the kind of part-time students' support group favoured by the Open University is unlikely to operate effectively in small degree programmes. In the evenings part-time student numbers are greater. This follows inevitably from the need for such programmes to be free standing.

What we see here are two quite different models of part-time provision. First is the freestanding or special part-time version of a degree programme, possibly available in the daytime or day and evening mode, but most likely to be available on an evening only basis. Here part-time students mix and learn with other part-timers and, in the case of evening only provision, with those staff prepared or required to work 'unsocial' hours. On the other hand, we have an additional model of a full-time degree to which a small number of part-time students is added. In the latter case the reference group must be the full-time student (and staff) culture into which the part-time student must fit. How easily this fit will be achieved will depend in part on the nature of the full-time student body. The greater emphasis in the polytechnics upon mature, non-standard entry students makes their full-time students rather more like part-time students on similar degrees. There is nothing surprising about the existence of these two models, but it is interesting that the models relate to different sectors of provision with most universities (and colleges of higher education) offering a single model.

Someone seeking the support of other part-time students on a daytime degree would be sensible to look towards the polytechnics. If it was felt to be more invigorating to mix with full-time students, either sector would do. However, if the only available degree which you wish to do in your local area is at a university and you do require the support of other mature part-time students, you might be better served by the Open University which will at least put you in touch with a network of similarly placed students. Those restricted to evening only study will be obliged to join a larger group.

Table 3.3   Mean number of first-year part-time students by mode of attendance

	Daytime	Evening	Day and evening	All	N =
Universities					54
Mean	7.1	28.3	32.1	16.4	
Standard deviation	9.9	12.2	53.0	26.4	
Polytechnics					124
Mean	19.3	32.9	33.3	24.3	
Standard deviation	21.6	24.0	25.5	23.5	
Colleges of higher education					37
Mean	24.1	19.5	11.0	21.9	
Standard deviation	17.3	14.2	1.4	16.0	
Scottish public sector					
Mean	18.0	36.8	–	28.7	
Standard deviation	7.2	31.0	–	24.5	
All institutions					222
Mean	17.3	29.2	31.5	22.1	
Standard deviation	19.4	20.8	35.5	23.3	

The availability of part-time courses is even more constrained when we look at the subjects offered. Tight (1986) identified only one evening only degree in engineering and only 13 in science, of which over a third were in mathematics. It is perhaps symptomatic of the skewed nature of evening provision that the same number of degrees were available in computing, engineering and in theology. Of course, in engineering the vast majority of part-time courses are BTEC higher certificate diploma courses (Department of Education and Science 1985a). Similarly in business studies, three-quarters of students are enrolled on professional courses rather than degree programmes *per se*. The development of Credit Accumulation and Transfer Schemes (CATS) and the Open Polytechnic may alter this.

Progress and survival

An issue which has tended to dominate the debates between the providers of part-time degrees is that of wastage. The wastage rates for part-time degrees are undoubtedly higher on average than for full-time courses. Not that 'wastage' is an appropriate term, particularly where part-time students are concerned. Many who leave subsequently return to some kind of academic or professional study. Many who leave do so for reasons peripheral to the course and its content. Others leave because mere attendance on the course achieves for them the very career advancement that they are seeking. Those who do leave because they cannot cope with or do not enjoy the course may nevertheless gain from the experience. What is more, with the development of CATS schemes such candidates can receive acknowledgement for whatever achievements they have obtained. For all these reasons, the term wastage is falling out of current usage, to be replaced with non-completion. Non-completion rates on part-time degrees are notoriously difficult to calculate. Unlike full-time degree programmes where the majority of the students complete the course in successive years, many part-time students spread their education over a longer period, sometimes moving between institutions. What is more the point at which comparisons are made is crucial for part-time programmes in a way that it is not for full-time programmes. Part-time programmes tend to have numbers of students who drop out in the first one or two weeks and never register. There is also considerable variation between institutions in the method of calculating non-completion rates after the first year of study.

Despite these difficulties the study of non-completion rates is fascinating. Our own data are based on course tutors' responses, on which we have no objective check. The alternative would be to seek the information from course reports prepared internally (and for the Council for National Academic Awards in the case of its institutions). However such reports are prepared with one eye on the internal distribution of resources and the other on external validation, so they are unlikely to be more reliable. The data obviously represent only those who responded. Of our respondents, over half of those from universities failed to answer this particular question compared with only one-quarter from the polytechnics. We have no way of knowing whether that non-response rate arises from university tutors not knowing the details or not being prepared to divulge them.

Methodological difficulties aside, the results are interesting. The findings are reported only for first year non-completion rates (Table 3.4). There are two main reasons for this. On almost all part-time degrees most drop out occurs in the first year. Secondly, first year rates are the most reliable and most readily comparable. Different institutions and even different departments within the same institution use different methodologies and different cut off points to calculate non-completion rates in subsequent years.

Our findings reveal differences by mode of attendance and by subject studied. The mean first year non-completion rate for all daytime courses was 16.9 per cent compared with 23.2 per cent for day and evening and 25.4 per cent for evening only courses. It would seem that a student's chances of survival are enhanced by daytime attendance. This is hardly surprising given the exigencies of evening attendance. The figures also suggest that survival chances on evening only courses are better in the university sector. However, some care must be taken in interpreting this since half the university respondents failed to reply to the question. Nevertheless, there may be substance to this observation, given the wide disparity in funding between the sectors (Chapter 4). What is worth noting about these figures is that they are markedly better than many practitioners have supposed. In our discussions

Table 3.4   First-year non-completion rates by mode of attendance

	Daytime	Evening	Day and evening	All	Non-response rate (%)	N =
Universities						30
Mean	16.0	15.3	15.2	15.7	53.8	
Standard deviation	8.0	13.9	12.3	9.8		
Polytechnics						192
Mean	17.9	30.9	26.9	21.7	27.0	
Standard deviation	17.6	20.3	16.2	18.6		
Colleges of higher education						24
Mean	13.8	26.2	8.0	17.7	35.1	
Standard deviation	8.8	27.2	–	17.6		
Scottish public sector						6
Mean	19.1	13.3	–	16.2	20.0	
Standard deviation	12.0	8.6	–	9.9		
All institutions						152
Mean	16.9	25.4	23.3	19.7	35.3	
Standard deviation	14.9	20.8	15.8	16.9		

with course tutors, with HMI inspectors and with members of the CNAA we consistently found assumptions that non-completion rates were worse than this. What is more they compare quite favourably with recent estimates for non-completion rates of full-time degrees (Johnes and Taylor 1989). Johnes and Taylor are quoted as claiming that: '(T)he average dropout rate from higher education is about 18 per cent. The figure is pushed up by numbers leaving polytechnics and colleges; the average university loses only 14.4 of its undergraduates before finals' (*Observer*, November 1989). These are total non-completion rates and we must be wary of direct comparisons with our first year rates, though most drop out occurs in the first year on full-time courses as well as on part-time.

The same articles show wide variations between institutions and between subjects studied. Among universities, for example, Dundee, Herriot-Watt, Glasgow, London, and Aberdeen were all reported to have an overall non-completion rate of 20 per cent or higher for their 1981 cohort, whereas Durham (6.1 per cent), Oxford (7.9 per cent), Loughborough (8.1 per cent), and York (8.6 per cent) all had low rates. We did not directly compare institutions but we did compare first year non-completion rates by subject studied (Figure 3.1). It is clear from this that the subject studied is a factor in student survival. The non-completion rate for law is more than twice the average for other subjects, though this tends to be mirrored to a lesser extent in full-time law degrees. What is perhaps more surprising to observe is the consistency of the

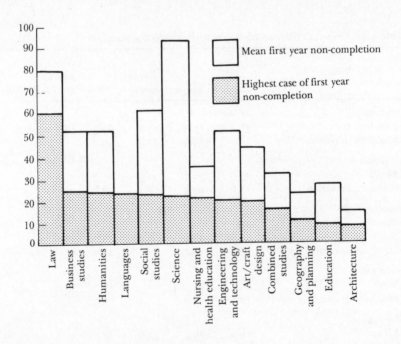

Figure 3.1   First year non-completion rates by subject.

figure across subject boundaries. The difference between the mean average rate and the worst case within each subject area is far greater than any differences between the means of different subject areas. While the average non-completion rate for science degrees was 20.9 per cent (comparable with other disciplines), one science degree admitted to a first year rate of 91 per cent. Even in law, there is a marked difference between the mean (57.0 per cent), the worst case (77.5 per cent) and the best (43.3 per cent). These differences between courses are of particular concern because part-time students necessarily have limited choice between courses within subject areas. Where they live may be the crucial factor in the subsequent success or failure of a student to the extent to which it determines their choice of institution and degree.

Quality of degree performance

The traditional view of the standards of part-time degrees has been less than complimentary. The emphasis in many institutions upon good 'A' level entry tends to devalue the contribution of the non-standard entry part-time student. Yet the quality of educational provision is surely better measured by its product than its input (Robinson 1988). Indeed, in speaking to potential employers one often finds an assumption that the difficulty of part-time study means that such students are potentially even better than their final grades might suggest. Certainly part-time study does involve real hardship for many people. However, there are other factors which may affect results. A study at Oxford Polytechnic related the performance in assignments of, mainly full-time, students to the number of students taking each module (Lindsay and Paton-Saltzberg 1987). The presence of large numbers of students did not increase the failure rate but it did appear to lower the average marks obtained. Although these results are for modular degree students not part-time students, the researchers' explanation that resources are the key issue is relevant for the study of part-time provision. Given what we know of part-time student numbers and their resourcing (Chapter 4), we might assume that part-time students' results are likely to be poor.

In fact, the results reported for part-time degrees were better than we had anticipated. Figure 3.2 presents the percentage classification results for all degrees in our survey by subject studied for the period 1982–85. Where there is no honours option available, the results are shown *below* the line as a proportion of all graduates. Where honours are available, the results are shown *above* the line as a proportion of total honours graduates. It should be stressed that we are only able to report results for those degrees which have graduated students. Most of the newer degrees include an honours classification so that the proportion of part-time students obtaining honours degrees should rise substantially in the near future.

The findings show some interesting trends. Straightforward professional/vocational subjects are more likely to graduate students without honours.

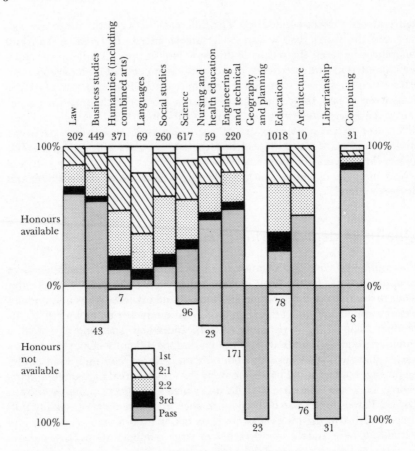

Figure 3.2   Class of part-time degree by subject.

Librarianship, architecture, business studies, law, computing, engineering and geography and planning all have large proportions of non-honours graduates. Education, also strongly professional in orientation, does not. Clearly these differences relate to professional requirements rather than the standard of degree work involved. Languages had by far the highest proportion of first class graduates, though the overall number of language students is very small and most language degrees have but a handful of part-time students. The next most successful by these criteria were science degrees.

Where honours were available, part-time degrees compared well with their full-time equivalents in all subjects. Whatever the increased difficulties of part-time study there is no evidence here of a second rate educational service. Nevertheless, differences by subject should not be ignored. Law, in particular, stands out from other part-time degrees in having a higher non-completion rate, a higher proportion of non-honours graduates and an average poorer class of degree. While none of this is likely to deter people wishing to enter the graduate profession by a part-time route, it might be valuable for law degree tutors in general to look closely at their practices.

Conclusions

Part-time students are not a homogeneous group and this needs to be reflected in the provision for them. They are diverse culturally, socially and in terms of lifestyle and life chances. The part-time student differs from the conventional 18-year-old, so favoured by policy makers, who once accepted on a degree is on a tramway to the terminus named graduation. There is a choice of routes or modes of study for the part-time student, the success of which provides a context within which conventional pedagogy and practices can be reassessed. This includes the when and how of study as well as the content and its appraisal. Part-time higher education, by the very nature of its practice, leads to a questioning of accepted values in higher education, of its organization, of the client group from which intergenerationally it reproduces itself of the value of the knowledge it imparts and, not least, of the amount and organization of its time. It reflects a wider concern about the nature and distribution of work in industrial societies (Department of Education and Science 1985b). The provision of evening only degrees, and also day-release courses, were responses to changes in individuals' time patterns. The extension of 'access' provision, the new emphasis upon mixed mode provision and the development of Credit Accumulation and Transfer Schemes (CATS) are further evidence of the flexibility of response (National Advisory Body/University Grants Committee 1988a; National Advisory Body/University Grants Committee 1988b). These are issues to which we will return in Chapter 5.

The balance of our findings presented so far clearly shows that there is a need for better guidance of both educators and potential part-time students. Prospective students have access to information services in the form of the Educational Credit Courses and Transfer Information Service (ECCTIS) and publications listing available courses (i.e. Tight 1990). Both of these provide an important service. However, hardly any of the part-time students on our own programme had used or even heard of these sources of information. Furthermore, these do not provide some of the key information which might be of value to potential students, like non-completion rates or average degree classifications of programmes. We observed that there were wide disparities in the performance of some degrees. The increasing 'market orientation' of higher education may encourage those institutions and degree programmes who believe that they have better records to publish their part-time degree results. This is already beginning to happen. It could enable students to make a more rational choice between the local university or polytechnic, or the Open University.

Better dissemination of information could also be crucial to improving both the appropriateness of provision and the level of performance of the providing institutions. In recent years there has been a genuine increase in provision. Yet we still find that provision is piecemeal, patchy and occasionally misinformed. We came across a number of part-time courses which had been launched but then withdrawn for lack of demand, some never having recruited a student. Such testing of the waters is likely to get short shrift from institutional management in the future. However, demand studies are notoriously difficult to effect. There is a danger that unless coherent strategies are developed at a national level, whether by government agencies or by interest groups, institutions will not risk innovative part-time developments. There is reason to hope that the proposed Open Polytechnic may go some way towards diminishing these misgivings by offering a framework within which the less experienced can operate. However, its organizers have already made it very clear that the Polytechnic will not be available to the university sector, where experience is least. More encouraging in this respect is the existence of the Polytechnic Association for Continuing Education (PACE) and the Association for Part-time Higher Education (APHE), both of which offer information services to members.

Part-time higher education has been a source of a wide range of innovatory practices. Distance learning, written course work material, the provision of audio – and video – material, skills-related learning, accreditation for previous experience, credit accumulation and transfer have all been practices which have operated within part-time provision and are now being looked at afresh by the higher education system as a whole. Associations of teachers devoted to the dissemination of good practice already exist in some disciplinary groups; but much might be gained from considering problems in a cross-disciplinary context.

There is a wide diversity of performance from existing degrees. While disseminating best practices should improve overall performance, one of the difficulties we observed was the relative isolation of course tutors (the ground troops of part-time provision). Isolation may encourage complacency. Before we published our comparative findings on performance we were frequently told by some practitioners that n failure rate or n non-completion rate was inevitable 'because they were part-time students'. A considerable amount of interest has recently been expressed in the development of performance indicators for a range of educational activity. Warwick University, for example, has attempted to produce a *Continuing Education Audit* (1987). On the whole such attempts are to be welcomed. The material presented here on non-completion rates, and success rates, and in subsequent chapters on costs, time and organization, offer criteria against which performance can be compared. Serious thought should be given to the development of better performance indicators and their dissemination to the relevant personnel.

4 | The Costing and Financing of Part-time Degree Provision

In this chapter we continue with our examination of first degree level part-time provision. Although government planning for the development of higher education assumes an increase in part-time degree level student numbers (Department of Education and Science 1985b; Department of Education and Science 1986a), the detailed proposals for funding full-time student numbers (Department of Education and Science 1988a) have not been matched by proposals for part-time student numbers (Smith and Saunders 1989b). Part-time higher education, other than that offered at the Open University which is under the direct surveillance of the Treasury, has been seriously neglected in cost–benefit calculations and in strategic planning. In this chapter we will look in detail at how part-time first degree provision is financed by both the providing institutions and the state.

To understand the way in which part-time provision is costed we must recognize that its development in the Polytechnic and Colleges Funding Council (PCFC) sector and in the universities has been largely unplanned. It has been a product of a variety of local initiatives, based upon a mixture of educational commitments to access and community and pragmatic responses to changes in educational policy. The calculation of the costs and benefits of higher education has normally been based on the full-time student and course as the base units and often appears to operate counter to an assumed financial rationality on the part of the providers. For example, until December 1986 public sector evening only provision was supported by the National Advisory Body (NAB) at a rate of 0.2 FTES (full time equivalent students). The NAB then increased the rate to 0.4 FTES, at which it has remained under the PCFC. This increase was merely indicative since it was not matched by any increase in overall resources, nor were resources necessarily distributed internally by institutions on this basis. The University Grants Committee (UGC) for its part urged universities not to distinguish between full- and part-time students. This appears to imply some kind of pro rata basis but since the UGC, now the University Funding Council (UFC), has not so far financed degrees on an hours–input basis the commitment lacks clarity.

There have been two consistent themes in government policy for funding higher education in recent years. One is the emphasis on support for science, technology and engineering; the other has been the attempt to bring higher education more into line with market forces. Recent proposals on the level and proportion of income generated by fees, and the process of assessing student costs, involve a reduction of bureaucratic allocation and state subsidy and a move towards deregulation. The demand is that higher education should become more cost effective. The promotion of market features in a state subsidized monopoly, it is alleged, will produce that effectiveness. One objective is to work towards a more market-determined price for the educational product. With this in mind the Universities Funding Council is inviting universities to bid for funded students in 1994–95 at or below a set of offer prices specified by the Council. The onus will be on the institutions to generate more output for the same or less financial input from the funding body. This will apply to both the funding of courses and of the students themselves. A recent decision to introduce four fee bands for students is intended by the government to be 'economically neutral'. Since fees for full-time students are normally paid by local authorities and the monies allocated for this purpose will be proportionately increased, this should be so. However, there will inevitably be ramifications for part-time students in this move (Smith and Saunders 1989b).

In June 1989 the PCFC made a number of proposals which overtly acknowledged the importance of part-time provision and were intended to encourage expansion. The document, 'Recurrent Funding Methodology 1990 –91: Guidance for Institutions', placed part-time provision within the mainframe of its planning exercise and revised funding methodology (PCFC 1989b). It introduced contract funding consisting of two elements: core funding based on a percentage of the previous year's allocation; and a component for which institutions will bid competitively. The latter allows an institution to propose a 'price' to the Council at which it would enrol students in addition to its core numbers, within each of nine programme areas. The methodology disaggregates full-time, sandwich and part-time numbers, with institutions bidding separately in each category both for core numbers and additional numbers. Within each category each whole student will count as *one*, rather than as a fraction of an FTES. This is intended to clarify and so enable comparison between the costs of full-time, sandwich and part-time students, while providing a measure of protection for part-time students from the worst effects of the new fee structure.

The absence of impact statements detailing the consequences of government financial initiatives has weakened the basis for sustaining support and development of part-time provision. The move from maintenance grants to a system of loans/grants may well alter the relationship between full- and part-time study. The recent achievement of an additional 50,000 student places, plus proposals for an extra 39,000 part-time places by 1995, does not mean any necessary comparable increase in income. The ability of institutions to cope with proposed increases in numbers and a more competitive market orientation will depend, in part, on their own methods of costing their part-time provision and therefore their assessment of the profitability of different modes of provision. What exists currently in the absence of national planning are different local methods developed on an *ad hoc* basis. One of our primary concerns has been to identify the range of local practices and attempt to codify them. Others (Rumble 1980) have looked in detail at distance learning and its costs. We concentrate on part-time provision within the universities, polytechnics and colleges of higher education. It is important to remember that distance learning and other forms of provision are competing in overlapping markets and that it is necessary or at least wise for each to take cognizance of the practices of the other. The recent development of the Open Polytechnic will make the competition even more direct.

The development of distance learning in Britain and elsewhere has stimulated a considerable amount of research into its relative cost. In part this has arisen out of the inadequacy of some of the initial forecasting. It also stems from the particular cost structure of distance learning, the initial fixed costs of which, unlike conventional courses, are greater than their variable costs (Laidlaw and Layard 1974). Even so, some studies may mislead in that they compare the costs of distance learning (part-time) with conventional learning which is full-time. Such comparisons have made the British Open University appear very economical (Wagner 1977). However, a study in Japan which compared distance learning directly with other part-time provision found the costs to be much the same (Muta 1985).

In the remainder of this chapter we look first at the level of institutional financial support for part-time programmes, both in terms of FTES weighting and calculated costs, as well as the fees charged to part-time students which were current at the time of our national survey. We then identify a number of ideal typical models of institutional funding for part-time degrees and examine the implications that the adoption of these different models have both for the institutions' own planning and policy and for national planning and policy.

National costings and part-time provision

Successive governments have centrally funded higher education through a system of bureaucratic allocation based upon national weightings in terms of FTES (full-time equivalent students). However, the national weighting of students varies between sectors, every student place being funded through the institution which the student attends. At the time of our survey the distinction between day and evening only students persisted, so that in the public sector the weighting varied even within the sector. More significantly, within the official categories there was considerable variation in actual practice. Table 4.1 shows the actual weighting of students employed, as reported by the course tutors. The mean weighting of university part-time students was 0.75 FTES for daytime and 0.77 for evening only students. A small number of day–evening courses reported a lower weighting of 0.41. This is more in keeping with the official public sector weighting. The actual figures for polytechnics and colleges of higher education give daytime students slightly less than their

Table 4.1   FTES weighting by sector and mode of attendance

	Daytime only	Evening only	Day and evening	All
Universities				
Mean	0.75	0.77	0.41	0.70
Standard deviation	0.26	0.17	0.18	0.26
Polytechnics				
Mean	0.39	0.24	0.36	0.35
Standard deviation	0.10	0.11	0.11	0.12
Colleges of HE				
Mean	0.32	0.25	0.40	0.34
Standard deviation	0.06	0.09	0.00	0.09

official weighting (0.38) and evening only students slightly more (0.25). It is argued by some in the PCFC sector that the actual difference in funding between sectors is greater than this since the universities are funded on a block grant system which appears to give them a higher unit of resource (Rickett 1987). The separation of teaching and research allocations will highlight this and may well reduce the difference.

The other major source of income to fund part-time provision comes from the charging of fees. Unlike most full-time undergraduates, part-time students are responsible for paying their own fees. In the past fees in the public sector were kept low as a matter of policy. There was also a good record of public sector and private sector employers supporting their employees in pursuit of part-time qualifications. Financial stringency has now hit the public sector badly and many private sector employers are less than enthusiastic about the government's call for them to contribute to economic fees. Some large companies, like Ford and BP, have part-time study policies but smaller companies have fewer resources. The reasons given for lack of support range from expense to fear of demands for higher salaries from those with enhanced credentials to the poaching activities of other firms, especially those from abroad which are able to pay better salaries. One might see this as a mercantilist approach to education and training: keep what you have got and take the best from others. On the positive side, however, in some subject areas

Table 4.2   Fees by sector (£, 1986)

	Mean	Standard deviation	Number of courses
Universities	231	106	59
Polytechnics	175	81	98
Colleges of HE	193	88	33

private employers, and of course professional bodies, have developed courses in conjunction with local institutions. How much they have contributed to the actual development costs is another matter.

It is plain that there are wide variations in fee levels between the sectors of provision (Table 4.2). University degree courses were the most expensive, with an overall mean (in 1985–86) of £231. Next came colleges of higher education with a mean of £193 and lowest were the polytechnics with mean annual fee of £175. The fees quoted are annual fees. Different types of degrees are of different lengths, so the actual cost to a student of a whole degree could vary from three to seven times this figure. Where degrees were modular and fees were charged per module we have calculated an appropriate annual fee. Comparisons with the Open University are difficult because its students typically take a longer time to graduate but an approximate comparison might be obtained, we would suggest, by multiplying the fee per course by three times. In the same year as our survey was conducted this would give a comparable 'annual' fee of £456 (excluding summer school).

In the past, within the then public sector, fees have normally been set according to a formula based on the number of contact hours, though where the course is specifically designed for a single employer it might be higher. No such system has operated for universities, though most appear to base fees pro rata on full-time fees. The structure and cost of provision varies by subject with some subjects charging substantially more than others. This might reflect the Department of Education and Science's view that some subjects are more expensive to teach than others because they require expensive facilities and equipment. Almost certainly the colleges of higher education fee level is influenced by the dominance of in service BEd degrees in their provision. However, this does not explain the higher university fee, since universities provide hardly any part-time degrees in 'expensive' science and engineering subjects.

Fee income has represented a small part of the income which institutions derive from their part-time provision. However, it will probably become increasingly important. The increased fee component for full-time students, reflecting a fee structure which more closely reflects actual costs, is likely to have a knock on effect for part-time students, despite assurances from the government to the contrary. The new market orientation underlying the restructuring of the funding bodies is already leading to a hiking up of fees. The effect of such rises is uncertain and will probably be differentially felt by subject area. If the Open University experience is anything to go by it is unlikely to dramatically affect overall demand but it may well restructure it, placing more emphasis on the employer rather than the student as client.

Institutional costing and part-time provision

The national system for the central allocation of funding in higher education operates differently for each sector of provision. The Open University and the

University Funding Council (previously the University Grants Committee) institutions receive a block grant to support a given programme of courses and enrolments, though small amounts are separately identified for special projects. In the case of some universities this includes reference to projections of anticipated numbers of part-time students. In the Polytechnic and Colleges Funding Council sector finance is directly related to the number of FTES allowed in each subject area. Given that part-time provision appears to be expensive it is generally assumed that it requires to be supported in some way. We sought in our survey to investigate this by asking respondents what was their estimated cost per student per year.

To our initial surprise the vast majority of our respondents did not know. Some 22 per cent of those in colleges of higher education claimed to know their costs, compared with only 9 per cent of those in polytechnics and 8 per cent of those in universities. As one university respondent told us, 'the university has not so far considered it necessary to assess costs of individual courses'. It was most surprising in the polytechnics where NAB funding levels were both public knowledge and somewhat parsimonious. The second surprise was that those who did claim to know offered us figures which varied enormously. For example, two virtually identical degrees in different institutions were costed at £335 and £995 per student respectively. The most expensive degree reported a cost of £4,700 per student.

Our first reaction was to blame the construction of our questionnaire. On further enquiry it became clear that the response realistically described the position of many course tutors. Both the lack of knowledge of many of those responsible for courses and the vast differences in the estimates of costs from those who did claim to know arose not just from ignorance or incompetence but from the range of practices adopted by institutions in assessing the costs of part-time provision.

Models of institutional funding

While most of the considerable and sustained growth in the part-time provision outside the Open University has been in what was the public sector (now the PCFC sector), more universities are also taking up the banner of continuing and part-time education. The speed of growth and the lack of national planning has led to uneven developments not just between institutions but also within the same institution. Thus we find some either lack a coherent policy or have different policies, coherent or otherwise, pursued side by side in different faculties or departments. We identified a number of distinct models of funding provision. Some refer to whole institutions and others to particular departments. In any case, they are ideal types, which are unlikely to be found applied universally within a single institution in pure form. Nevertheless, they are instructive.

Model A: funding at FTES

Model A involves the funding of part-time education in proportion to the FTES accorded to its students. It is the model on which central planning, such as it is, has assumed institutions to be operating. The number of FTES is a factor in determining institutional funding, especially in the PCFC sector, where each part-time student is worth two-fifths of a full-time student. We found very few public sector degrees which operated at FTES funding levels. It was more likely for day only or for day–evening courses and especially modular programmes where the number of units could be adjusted to match the weighting (though with a subsequent extension of the time taken to complete the degree). Where historically this model has presented the most difficulty has been with evening only provision in the public sector (where at the time of our survey each student was worth only one-fifth of the full-time equivalent). In the survey we did find a very few examples of evening only degrees costed at FTES but these tended to operate on the basis of mass lectures only. In the university sector more evening only degrees appear to use this model, though the FTES rate used is an internal one which was set at four times the public sector rate (0.8 compared with 0.2 in 1985–86). This model tends to discourage the development of free standing part-time degrees though it may not discourage the extension of part-time access to full-time degrees.

Model B: acknowledged subsidy

This model of institutional part-time costing openly acknowledges the inadequacies of FTES funding levels and offers a direct subsidy to part-time students. Thus a 0.4 FTES student might be recosted for internal purposes at, say, 0.5 FTES. This model operates on free standing part-time degrees which institutions recognize as being under-resourced at the official level. The model has the advantage that all parties know precisely the amount of subsidy which goes towards part-time provision. For the part-time degree there is clarity of budgeting and for the institution a clear indication of other programmes' contribution to supporting part-time provision. It also allows for the financial implications of any new part-time developments to be seen in advance. However, the model is strongly dependent upon the methodology of course costing (see below) and is not extensively used at present.

Model C: departmental fudge

Many institutions devolve a lot of academic planning decisions to the departmental level. Funds are allocated to departments, which, as long as they operate within required limits have a degree of autonomy in how they allocate their resources. It is the popularity of this model which explains why so few part-time course tutors knew the subsidy which they received. Within this model departments tend to distribute resources, especially teaching staff, in terms of what needs to be done to keep the programmes going. There are clear advantages in these arrangements for part-time provision, since in practice they tend to hide and therefore exclude from debate the cost of that provision. This is particularly the case where part-time students are slotted into full-time degree programmes. Indeed, it is relatively unusual to find this model operating in anything like its pure form with independent part-time degrees. It is in the nature of fudging that procedures are imprecise, lacking explicitness and coherence. In terms of how the model typically operates this is probably a fair description. However, there are moves to firm up this model with the use of more precise costings of the various inputs and the value of outputs. This is most clearly expressed in the concept of cost centres. A cost centre is a level of organization to which responsibility is devolved. Where the cost centre is the department it differs little from fudge. Where it is more broadly defined, as for example the faculty, this allows for more open and, it is hoped, constructive debate about the allocation of resources (Kail 1988).

Model D: bias factor model

An interesting development which is being applied in a few institutions is the bias factor model of part-time costing. This is an extension of the subsidy model in that rather than offering specific subsidies to specific programmes it seeks to identify universal weightings for part-time students in relation to overall institutional funds, based on their equivalence to full-time resourcing. As long as the bias factor is greater than 1.0 then a subsidy is being effected. The advantages of this model over model B is that in this case all part-time provision engaged in by a faculty, department or programme will be subsidized prior to the central distribution of funds. This then operates as a reward system for recruiting part-time students. Indeed, to the extent that it continues to operate the bias factor is a constant inducement to expand part-time numbers in a way that the subsidy model is not.

Methodologies of cost calculation

Whichever model is in operation the assumed cost of supporting part-time provision will depend upon the methodology of cost calculation adopted by the institution. No consistent methodology is employed by institutions, even within the same sector of provision and it is variation in the methods of calculation rather than any actual real differences in the use of resources which probably accounts for our questionnaire responses. The detailed methodologies are extremely complex and appear not to be properly understood even by those whom they directly affect. Like any uniform technique a costing mechanism may be required to assist in the attainment of several policy objectives. A form of calculation which works for the institution as a whole or for a specific purpose may not produce similarly satisfactory results for different, coexisting or conflicting purposes.

There are three common methods of calculation which are applied to part-time provision. The first is full cost calculation. Here it is argued that part-time provision should accept its fair share of all costs. As long as institutions were funded as wholes it was reasonable to offset income against cost in terms of FTES or some similar basis of comparison. This method tends to make part-time provision look relatively expensive unless it is limited to small numbers of part-time students taking parts of full-time courses as in daytime modular programmes. The second is a form of marginal cost calculation. Here it is argued that since part-time students often use facilities at times when full-time students do not – evenings, Saturday mornings, Wednesday and Friday afternoons – they incur minimal additional central costs and so should be costed on the marginal cost of their provision. This might include library, porterage and catering in the evenings plus electricity and heating charges, as well as the cost of teaching. The third common method is an alternative version of marginal cost calculation. Here, it is argued that part-time provision is in addition to standard provision, which itself should cover the running costs of the institution. Thus part-time provision should be costed in terms of the actual costs of teaching and administration only. Given that many evening part-time courses make extensive use of part-time staff, who are markedly cheaper, this makes part-time degrees appear very good value for money.

Irrespective of the lavishness or otherwise of the provision, any degree may appear expensive, reasonable or cheap, according to which method of calculating costs is applied.

Funding models and their impact upon institutional policy and planning

We have identified four models of costing part-time provision. Each represents a perfectly viable and understandable response to the difficulties of funding part-time provision. Each model has specific implications for the way an institution operating it will view its part-time provision. It will also influence an institution's capacity to recognize and respond to changes in national policy and the market for part-time students. We will consider each model in turn in relation to the present method of funding higher education.

Model A

This model is most commonly to be found in the university sector. A particular form of it operated within the University of London until recently. Though the financial crisis which affected Birkbeck College now appears to have been resolved (Birkbeck College 1987), it points to the danger of the model, the rigidity of which allows no mechanism for responding to changing situations without abandoning the model itself.

In the PCFC sector this model has the advantage at one level of taking part-time provision out of the policy debate. As long as it accords with FTES it is not seen to be problematic. However, the traditional very low level of public sector FTES weighting, especially for evening only students, has created its own problems. There are degrees which appear to have operated at this level but only at the cost of high non-completion rates. Its danger is that it may marginalize the part-time student who may come to be seen as a top up to the budget or to the seminar group.

The model does, however, have implications for an institution's ability to plan part-time programmes coherently. By making part-time education non-problematic it also removes the focus for policy initiatives deriving from central management, which may become restricted to mere exhortations. Any more determined efforts to influence course provision tend to lead to the adoption of an alternative model. The popularity of this model may increase under the proposed new PCFC method of funding. However, the abandonment of FTES will not solve the problems unless the value of each part-time student is set relatively high, especially in relation to the bidding exercise for additional students.

Model B

This model in its present form is the most conducive to rapid and effective central planning. The operation of subsidies is generally an effective means of encouraging the expansion of part-time provision as well as an effective way of policing it. Since subsidies operate directly upon the degree they allow decisions to be made upon non-financial criteria – i.e. educational need, student demand or political expediency. This model is also the most efficient at engendering new areas of provision, even free standing degrees. The latter are difficult to initiate under alternative models because of the high initial investment, as in distance learning. The perceived need of institutions to rapidly and cheaply develop part-time provision has militated against the establishment of free standing part-time degrees where this model has not been operating.

One disadvantage of the model is that strong central directives may encourage part-time developments where the academics themselves have given low priority, and so may lead to problems of low morale. Also, given the present system of financing higher education, subsidies to part-time education must generally speaking be seen as financed from full-time provision. Subsidy may be used as a loss leader or to develop particular projects. It should be remembered, however, that subsidy is always a political decision and that the subsidy provided one year can be taken away the next. Nevertheless, we know of one institution which has successfully financed its part-time programme out of profits made elsewhere.

The greatest disadvantage to part-time education of this model appears to us to be its vulnerability to changes in the methodology of course costing. So, while the model probably provides the most effective way for institutions to expand their part-time provision in specific areas, it may also make them highly vulnerable to attack by other academics. Until we obtain the financial details, it is not possible to state the effect of the new PCFC funding method on this model. Certainly a low assessment of the financial value of a part-time student and the possibility of virement built into the new system would suggest its continuation.

Model C

All our researches point to the initiatives here arising at the departmental level. Having initially supported ventures into part-time provision, departments then find themselves saddled with maintaining them. From the departmental view there are many advantages in this model. It allows for the distribution of both teaching and administrative resources on the basis of need rather than FTES or managerial whim. However, it is also highly vulnerable to the idiosyncrasies of course costing methodologies if, and when, they are applied. Often, though, the nature of departmental fudge means that course costing – involving a critical look at the criteria of weighting and distribution – is never done. A proper assessment might involve disaggregation and the opening up of the books beyond departmental level. Formally, this is what the funding bodies, particularly the PCFC, are demanding.

This model also presents major problems for the coherent institutional planning of part-time provision. The model in its pure form requires the abrogation of responsibility by central management. Decisions on the maintenance, contraction or expansion of provision, short of major changes in departmental budgets, are all made at departmental level. This may lead to widely differing and even contradictory policies being pursued in different departments within the same institution. Apart from the desire for departmental independence some would advocate this diversity on the basis of letting sleeping dogs lie, i.e. it can fudge over potential conflict and give middle management a certain control over staff. Moreover, politically aware promoters of part-time provision who have innovated may fear a change to a more punitive methodology.

Model D

The bias factor model is a relatively new model and there is little experience of its operation. It has the advantages of the subsidy model in encouraging the development of part-time provision, without the disadvantages associated with some course costing methodologies. It also avoids the possible arbitrary application of the subsidy model in that it embodies a concept of 'fairness' across part-time provision. It is most effective in institutions committed to expansion which have as yet few part-time students. The built in notion of fairness assists in the mobilization of staff support since its impetus appears to be non-directive. It is designed to encourage development across the board. It may well therefore encourage inappropriate or ill suited provision in some departments.

There is also the danger of over-expansion with this model. Whilst those working in the field may feel expansion to be desirable *per se*, over-expansion has its dangers. It may subsequently become necessary to modify the model to ensure an appropriate mix of full-time courses, otherwise the quality of that provision may be affected. This model, then, allows for strong institutional control over the expansionist phase but not over its content or its distribution. As expansion progresses, central control becomes increasingly uncertain.

Responsiveness to national policy and planning

The different implications (see Table 4.3 for summary) which these models have for institutional planning will also be reflected in their responsiveness to national planning initiatives. For the purposes of illustration we will use the currently operated models of funding cognizant of the proposed changes. One important aspect of these proposals should be borne in mind. The hoped for expansion of part-time numbers is unlikely to be matched by increased real resources. Hence the offering prices set by the Funding Councils will be set

Table 4.3   Models and their implications

Type of funding	Influenced by costing methodology	Implications for institutional planning	Implications for government planning
Model A FTES funding	No influence	Neutral	Strong influence
Model B Acknowledged subsidy	Highly influenced	Strong institutional control	Ambiguous influence
Model C Departmental fudge	Influenced	Weak institutional control	Weak influence
Model D Bias factor	No influence	Ambiguous institutional control	Moderate influence

relative to their policy objectives and those of the providing institutions themselves. Any upgrading of part-time provision, without a corresponding increase in total resources, is likely to be at the expense of a reduction in the price of full-time provision.

With Model A any increase in FTES or the unit price would immediately release additional resources for part-time provision, which, it is hoped, might lead to an expansion in numbers and a reduction in non-completion rates. However, unless the increase were a substantial one it is unlikely that this would lead to new initiatives because of the high initial set up costs. Rather it would encourage the expansion of existing programmes.

Under Model B the impact would be more ambiguous. An increase in the external evaluation of FTES would certainly reduce pressure on such provision but unless the increase were such as to be greater than the subsidy it would be unlikely to have much impact upon programmes. An increase in quota numbers might have a more direct effect but this would again depend on whether the institution was prepared to offset an increase in subsidy against an increase in quota numbers. The conclusion reached might well depend upon which course costing methodology were used and hence how expensive the course appeared to be.

A national initiative would be least effective where Model C operated. While undoubtedly all institutions would be glad of the increase in funding which would go with improved FTES, since under this system departments distribute resources according to need rather than external weighting, this would not necessarily lead to redistribution of resources. It would be most likely to work in the PCFC sector where disaggregation has been proposed, since this would make fudging more difficult. However, other things being equal any decision by departments to expand provision is likely to be taken on the basis of other criteria. An increase in quota numbers, however, might encourage departments to increase numbers providing they could do so within existing or proposed resource levels. The marginal cost of a few extra bodies in a seminar may encourage taking more up to the point at which a further seminar group is required. Expansion beyond that point is unlikely under this model.

The adoption of model D would make institutions moderately receptive to government initiatives of the sort suggested. An increase in the FTES rating would require the bias factor to be recalculated and thus encourage a further expansion of part-time numbers. The problem with this model would arise in a period of stasis or decline in numbers.

Changes in the structure of financing higher education

Our analysis of the impact of national policy upon the different models was predicated upon the assumptions of the existing system. Some aspects of that model have not changed. The UGC and the NAB have not been replaced by a single body as many argued but by the UFC (University Funding Council) and the PCFC (Polytechnics and Colleges Funding Council). The transbinary

Model A Bureaucratic allocation: the funding of places

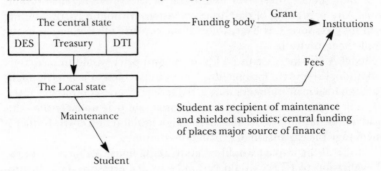

Model B Financial instruments and criteria of evaluation

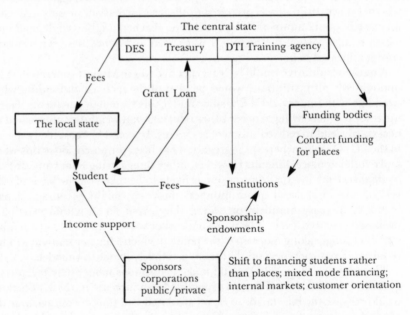

Figure 4.1   Changing structure of financing higher education.

divide remains, with continued differential funding for part-time students and problems for coherent national planning. However, in another sense the PCFC and the UFC represent a new structure for higher education funding. Government thinking, and to some extent action, is moving away from a state funded service model based on the bureaucratic allocation of resources (Model A in Figure 4.1) towards a new model (Model B in Figure 4.1). This new model is drawn from the principles of market economics. Whereas under the old system the archetypal student is a recipient of maintenance and shielded subsidies, the new model is more of a partnership based on competition and a reassertion of the rights and role of the client. There is, however, ambiguity as to whom is the client. The old system clearly focused on providing places, with the student as client (and recipient of a grant). Part-time students were different because they did not receive a grant. The new system encourages the role of sponsor both for individual students and for the institutions themselves, so the sponsor as well as the student is the client. However, the emphasis on the sponsor rather than the place diminishes the distinction between the full-time student and the part-time student. We can see the different emphasis which underlies these two models in both the allocation of funds to the institutions and in the allocation of funds to the students. Although they have been presented by the government and the funding bodies as separate issues, our diagram (Figure 4.2) clearly shows the connections.

Financing institutions: the role of fees

In April 1989 the government proposed a fundamental change to the mechanism for allocating support funds to institutions. The course fees, paid ostensibly by full-time students but in practice by their local authorities (who in turn are reimbursed by the government) should be increased by from 200 per cent to 300 per cent, while the direct grant to institutions would be reduced by a comparable amount. This was seen by the government as being economically neutral, since it paid the institutions directly for places and indirectly by the fee. The purpose of this change was to make students more economically aware by emphasizing the cost of their courses rather than to introduce any immediate change in the actual funding levels.

In the PCFC sector this was linked with a loosening of the guidelines on student numbers to allow institutions to increase their numbers beyond those centrally financed. The increased fee income per additional student was expected to encourage such practice and so encourage competition between institutions for markets. If the acquiescence of the Treasury to what appears open ended funding is surprising it need not be so. Should access increase, and institutions begin to charge a premium fee as some have suggested, there is nothing to prevent the Treasury then reducing overall funding and so forcing a reduction in the monies given directly by the funding bodies to the providing institutions. Indeed, there has even been discussion by the CVCP of the possibility of full cost fees.

It is possible that such a system will foster greater consumer satisfaction and institutional competitiveness, while reducing unit costs and increasing access, at least for full-time students. However, considerable fears exist about its impact upon part-time provision, which the Department of Education and Science itself has acknowledged as an element in the necessary expansion (see Chapter 2). It is clearly not the government's intention to undermine part-time provision. The Consultative Document specifically says that it will protect the funds available for part-time places in the PCFC sector, and looks to them:

> to recognize this feature in the grant paid to support those places. In these circumstances, there is no reason why part-time fees should rise, except as might in any case be appropriate between years.
>
> Department of Education and Science 1989

However, the new relationship between the PCFC and its institutions, with an emphasis on competitiveness and market forces, frees the polytechnics to increase their fees at will. The DES position also demonstrates a lack of understanding of the structure of much part-time provision, which is increasingly being developed within modular packages. Where part-time and full-time students are taking identical modules there must be a strong temptation to charge pro rata fees. Most universities have already adopted this practice.

While increased fees may not affect those in receipt of a mandatory grant and are not intended to affect part-time students, they are, in reality, likely to have an impact upon access. Many part-time and associate students study subjects which are unlikely to sustain high fees. The search for fee income may undermine such provision, replacing it with high status, high earning courses. The change in the balance of income between grant and fees may also discourage experimentation on the part of institutions. We calculate that the funding bodies could lose some 30 per cent (£70 million) of their income. This is secure income based on student FTES numbers which they know in advance. It will be replaced by student fee income dependent upon market forces. It is problematic whether or not institutions will be prepared to risk developing high cost-low income courses for minority markets in this context.

We have pointed out some of the unforeseen dangers. However, at this stage it is important to stress that these are only specifications. The system is untried. What is more, there are possible benefits to access, including part-time provision, which could arise. Let us summarize some of the possible consequences. First, institutions may find it more profitable to concentrate on full-time rather than part-time study. Even were the fees from both routes to be the same, the differential weighting of part-time students means that they are likely to be less revenue effective for the providing institution. Secondly, increases in full-time fees are likely to push up part-time fees. Much depends upon the income levels of prospective part-time students. For the better off there may well be an expansion of opportunities but appropriately costed and probably available during the day as part of modular schemes. For the less well off concentration on income generating courses may reduce the choice and what is available will probably be much more expensive than at present. Thirdly, institutions who are prepared and able to expand full-time courses in areas of high demand may be able to substantially increase their income levels. This raises the possibility of subsidizing part-time or access programmes as a service to the community, even possibly on a marginal costs basis. The possibilities are even greater where there are consortia. One Scottish college is already operating a system whereby surpluses are transferred to courses as part of a research, teaching and consultancy package.

Financing students: top-up loans

A new system of funding full-time students has been introduced as a result of the proposals of the Student Support Review Group. The issue here, as far as students are concerned, is the extent to which the level of mandatory grant has fallen behind the level of inflation. The issue from the government's point of view is the cost of finding even the existing level of grant, which in 1987 was estimated at £510 million or 20 per cent of the recurrent expenditure on higher education, and the need to engender a new market orientation in education. A variety of solutions were offered to the Review Group, ranging from the updating of the level of mandatory grant to the radical proposition first mooted by Sir Keith Joseph for a student voucher scheme which would shift the basis of financial support from the institution to the receiving student (see Figure 4.1). The group chose a compromise and entitled their paper 'Top-up Loans for Students' (Department of Education and Science 1988d). It proposed retaining the mandatory grant but permanently freezing it at the existing level, while offering interest-free loans to students to top up their income to a realistic level. These loans are to be updated annually, though on an assumption of a 3 per cent inflation rate (compared to an actual inflation rate at the time of 7 per cent). At the same time most students cease to be eligible for income support, unemployment benefit or housing benefit, though three 'access' funds (initially proposed at £5 million each, but subsequently reduced) would be created to assist with hardship.

Part of the logic of these proposals was to increase access to higher education. The government's own projections for increased student numbers, as we saw in Chapter 2, rely heavily on the assumption that mature students, and especially women, and those from ethnic minorities and lower social classes, will be seeking degrees in far greater numbers.

> If I had to make one projection for Higher Education, it is that in 25 years time women will be in the majority . . . and the number of students from ethnic minorities in Britain will increase both absolutely and proportionately.
>
> Baker 1989b

Whilst in a society used to living on credit it cannot be assumed that indebtedness will act as a deterrent, it can hardly be asserted that marginal students and those from minority groups with historically low participation rates will be encouraged by any loan scheme unless it is financed in a highly favourable way. The White Paper proposals have been criticized by the National Union of Students precisely because they discriminate against these type of students.

From the point of view of part-time study the White Paper was particularly depressing. Lobbying for part-time higher education had concentrated on persuading the government to make some contribution to their fees. In fact an early decision to exclude part-time students from consideration made this an unrealistic expectation. In any case it was seen as inappropriate to the notion of 'economic awareness', which was to be expressed in the payment of fees. In another sense, the White Paper proposals are irrelevant to part-time higher education. It is only in the context of the wider model (Figure 4.1) that their possible impact on part-time provision can be observed.

In fact, the likelihood of the White Paper proposals as such being implemented in their entirety remains in doubt. Even supporters of loan schemes are highly critical of the specific proposals (Barnes and Barr 1988). The banks have already declined to participate in the operation of the scheme which they see as possibly threatening to their already thriving student market. However, the minister has insisted that the proposals will be introduced, though it will require the government to spend substantial sums on its administration, thus detracting from one of the supposed advantages of the scheme. This is likely to have wider ramifications upon the funding of the system. On his appointment the Secretary of State for Education was adamant that higher education could not expect to win a significantly greater share of public spending in the future (MacGregor 1989b). The proposals have been damned by the Labour Party, though it has offered no alternative method of financing expansion to the system. Nevertheless the proposals are going forward.

If further problems do arise in passing the top-up loans scheme, and when the enormous cost becomes publicly obvious, it is possible that the Conservative Party will again raise the issue of student vouchers. Although this proposal, originating with Sir Keith Joseph, was not pursued, it should not be dismissed. So far vouchers have been discussed entirely within the context of full-time students. However there is no reason why a voucher or entitlement could not be granted to all citizens to be redeemed as and when they desired (see Chapter 5). Whether such schemes, based as they are on consumer preference, can improve quality or reduce costs is problematic, given the unpredictable nature of the demand.

Conclusions

If the assumptions about 'getting the economy right' are applied to higher education, it ought to be able in turn to contribute more effectively towards assisting the economy. Potential students will be better off and so better able to pay. The problem for potential part-time students is that the supposed trickle down effects of supply side policies may not happen for those groups already in the lower income brackets. There is a danger that the dual labour market will be reproduced in higher education. The primary labour market of those who are highly skilled, highly paid, often working in large successful firms, can demand more education as a condition of their employment and can afford to contribute towards high fees. The secondary labour market of those in small, low wage firms has little chance of sponsorship. Without state support it is doubtful that these people will be entering higher education, yet this is a group which the government is concerned to target in order to solve any coming manpower shortage.

The changes to the system of funding national provision have failed to recognize that there are different clients for part-time education. The government's assurances about protecting the funding of part-time provision are unconvincing in the context of large fee increases. The PCFC's provisional announcement of a 10 per cent increase in direct funding for part-time provision is to be welcomed. However, its proposals for incentives to institutions for the over-recruitment of part-time students are vague and seem to contradict its specific assurances that fees will be kept down. The likely increases in fees plus the institutional emphasis on income generation bode ill for the expansion of part-time provision unless the government takes seriously proposals for paying part-time students' fees.

Whatever form the national system of distribution of funding eventually takes our findings show that the method of internal resource distribution within institutions has an effect upon their view of the cost of their part-time provision. Particularly important is the methodology of costing adopted. Institutional managements should make themselves aware of the arbitrary elements in official costings which otherwise may inhibit their preparedness to develop part-time programmes. The methods of financial control and distribution adopted by institutions can also affect their responsiveness to national planning initiatives. Incentive schemes should take this into account.

5 | Educational Modes of Organization and Alternative Routes

In previous chapters we have related developments in part-time provision to the major agents of educational change in order to understand present and potential patterns of demand. In this chapter we will examine those educational facets of higher education which influence the direction of part-time routes.

Pollitt (1990) uses the term 'modernization' perspective to explore the tensions between the needs of contemporary society and the present structure of the system of higher education. His primary concern is with the failure of the university sector to respond to the need for demographically broader access and enhanced competence. This analysis could be extended to the polytechnics. While they have been much more flexible in responding to changing demands than have the universities, they also tend towards the conventional model of provision (Figure 3.1).

The defect of the modernization perspective is that it sees the system of higher education as in a crisis arising from its inability adequately to respond to social imperatives. As Hussain (1976) argues, the education system does not respond reflexively to external demands. Indeed the organization of learning expresses, in a condensed and mediated way, wider issues of social control and power (Bernstein 1971). Those who wish to develop or implement changes in higher education, including adult and continuing education, must understand 'the logic of the academy' (Williamson 1990). This logic is examined by Becher and Kogan (1980) in their model of 'how the components of higher education, and the system as a whole work'. In so doing, they stress, like Lockwood and Davis (1985), what is distinctive about the organization of higher education and the conflicts and diffusion of power operating at different levels of the system.

We would argue that, rather than higher education being in a state of crisis, present changes can be better interpreted dynamically as heralding a new stage of development. To examine the issues raised by this new stage we have developed an analytic framework (Figure 5.1) building upon the concept of a mode of educational organization. This framework identifies a number of factors which underpin different assumptions about the practices and purposes of higher education. Through it we can locate and explore organizational

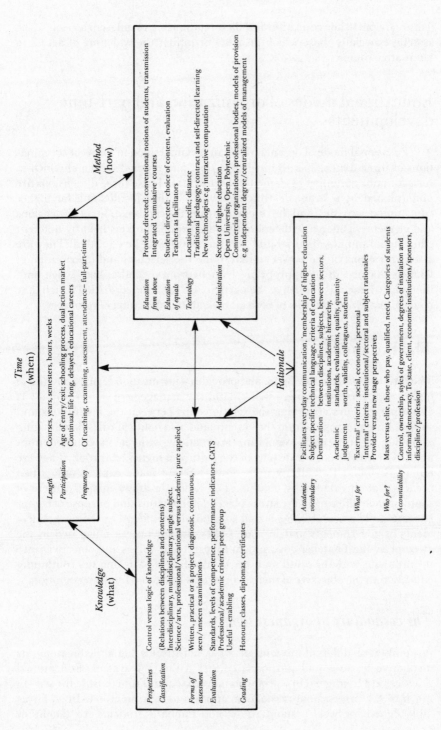

Figure 5.1 Descriptive model of educational modes of organization.

Time
(when)

Length	Courses, years, semesters, hours, weeks
Participation	Age of entry/exit; schooling process, dual action market Continual, life long, delayed, educational careers
Frequency	Of teaching, examining, assessment, attendance – full-part-time

Method
(how)

Education from above	Provider directed: conventional notions of students, transmission Integrated 'cumulative' courses
Education of equals	Student directed: choice of content, evaluation Teachers as facilitators
Technology	Location specific; distance Traditional pedagogy; contract and self-directed learning New technologies e.g. interactive computation
Administration	Sectors of higher education Open University, Open Polytechnic Commercial organizations, professional bodies, models of provision e.g independent degree/centralized models of management

Knowledge
(what)

Perspectives	Control versus logic of knowledge (Relations between disciplines and contents)
Classification	Interdisciplinary, multidisciplinary, single subject. Science/arts, professional/vocational versus academic, pure applied
Forms of assessment	Written, practical or a project, diagnostic, continuous, seen/unseen examinations
Evaluation	Standards, levels of competence, performance indicators, CATS Professional/academic criteria, peer group Useful – enabling
Grading	Honours, classes, diplomas, certificates

Rationale

Academic vocabulary	Facilitates everyday communication, 'membership' of higher education Subject specific technical language, criteria of education
Demarcation	between disciplines, subjects, between sectors, institutions, academic hierarchy,
Academic Judgement	standards, evaluations, quality, quantity worth, validity, colleagues, students
What for	'External' criteria: social, economic, personal 'Internal' criteria: institutional/sectoral and subject rationales Provider versus new stage perspectives
Who for?	Mass versus elite, those who pay, qualified, need, Categories of students
Accountability	Control, ownership, styles of government, degrees of insulation and informal democracy, To state, client, economic institutions/sponsors, discipline/profession

features of part-time education and their relationship to different aspects of the system, especially those which promote or inhibit the widening of access to alternative routes.

Educational modes of organization and part-time developments

An educational mode of organization can be understood in terms of combinations of three dimensions – knowledge, time and method – each of which in turn contains a number of elements (Figure 5.1). These three dimensions are underpinned by a rationale which provides both a justification for higher educational activities, and the rules governing the combinations of dimensions and elements. Different educational modes express notions held by different educational publics about ability and the capacity to be educated. They are also expressions of the power to determine the selection and distribution of what is deemed to be appropriate content from available knowledge and, therefore, the relative worth of the participants, and the education which they receive, expressed in terms of both status and the allocation of resources.

The Rationale

The rationale gives meaning to, and provides a justification of, the activities of higher education: teaching, research and the management of institutions. It encompasses rules governing the relationships between the institutions and subject bureaucracies within the system, and also political rules demarcating academic territories and regulating interactions with the external environment. These rules constitute part of the culture of higher education. They are not to be found formally written down but are made explicit only when breached or threatened by conflict. The rationale draws upon a variety of sources, each differing in the stress placed on the nature and purpose of higher education. The nearest we get to a societal view is found in the pronouncements of governments and in state policy documents, as illustrated in the attempt by the Thatcher government to insert new values and objectives into the rationale, with the result that the contribution of part-time and continuing education to the objective of increasing access has gained some recognition.

The vocabulary of organization

A number of different notions of what constitutes higher education, its distinctive features and purposes, coexist within the system. Educational practices are conducted in a professional vernacular. From outside the system much of the professional vernacular appears to lack precision. In so far as 'able', 'good', or 'weak', 'standard' or 'non-standard' students are 'taught' or 'learn' on 'subdegree', 'degree level' or 'postgraduate' 'courses' in different 'subjects' or 'subject areas' on a 'full-time' or 'part-time' basis and their 'progress' is 'monitored', 'examined' and 'graded' and 'research' undertaken, we have to assume that educational organizations and their practices have some internal coherence. These institutional categories are themselves inter-twined with the operational vocabulary of disciplines which contain value judgements and provide meaning for those professing them. Disciplinary values and beliefs may conflict with those of other disciplines and with those of the institution within which they are located. Even at the level of the subject department conflicts may arise both over different interpretations of the discipline and how it is communicated to students. Here professional egos are strongest.

The vocabulary of higher education also expresses judgement about the prestige of different institutions, their clients and their academic and research activities. Included here are evaluations, based on 'standards', of the suitabil-ity of individuals to enter and progress. The Universities Council for Adult and Continuing Education (UCACE) maintain that standards have been the greatest barrier to part-time study in the universities (Universities Council for Adult and Continuing Education 1990). While this conclusion refers to academic standards it could be extended to include a range of expectations about student behaviour and performances. Oleson and Whittaker (1968) refer to the process of socialization into a variety of occupations as a 'silent dialogue'. It is not surprising that the educational background and lifestyle of some part-time students makes it difficult for them to adequately master this silent dialogue with the implicit expectations of academic courses.

The rationale, selection and access

Institutions screen entrants – the more prestigious the institution, the tighter the criteria. This is usually undertaken on the basis of examination grades. Mace (1989) suggests that the demand for high grades might have more to do with the rationing of limited places than with the ability of candidates to succeed on the course. Moreover, there are subjective judgements as to the appropriateness of students to engage in the 'silent dialogue', and enhance the status of the institution. Applicants, and their schools and families, tend to share this notion of institutional status and suitability, in that for many candidates, status is a major criterion when applying for entrance. More significantly for expansion and democratization, large numbers define them-selves out. As Edwards puts it:

> The idea that intellectual excellence is confined to the mastery of abstract specialized disciplines and has no necessary direct relevance to the improvement of human life presents little difficulty to those from families familiar with the gamesmanship of entry to higher education. But it constitutes still another barrier of incomprehension, of mystery, to the

majority of the population for whom such games are as strange as the Eton Wall game.

Edwards 1982

Of the connection between social and educational background and organization, Edwards adds, 'It also provides an excellent reason for limiting entry permanently to a small fraction of the population' (Edwards 1982).

The relatively low participation rate does not mean that there are no contradictions and alternatives within the system. The expansion of part-time courses, the growing possibilities for continuing education and the fact that the numbers enrolled in adult education are estimated to be around 1.2 million (Department of Education and Science 1988b) illustrate viable alternatives to conventional perceptions and routes.

There are a number of perspectives, each vying to define what and who higher education is for and thus its forms of organization. These range from a Platonic and elitist view that only a minority are capable of engaging in 'high culture' and perpetuating excellence, to those who wish to widen access and reorganize around the precepts of continuing education. There is a democratic strand of humanist and often anti-vocationalist pedagogy here, exemplified by the late Raymond Williams, in which a critical intelligence has to be nurtured through an initiation into the products of common culture. One extension of this view is to argue that higher education should give back to the people what it has drawn from them and consolidated into academic subject bureaucracies (Hoare 1965). An important aspect of adult and continuing education has, therefore, been a concern with the development of the self of the learner (Knowles 1978; Jarvis 1989).

The extension of part-time routes to a wider clientele still faces barriers that are not just financial. There is a small yet significant conservative element which, fearing the emancipating potential of education, hopes that the insertion of market forces will restrict critical thought (Johnson 1989). They support the inclusion of new stake holders, especially commercial interests and consumers, and so seek changes in the locus of control. Their stress is on the more personal and utilitarian benefits of education, with particular emphasis on technical competence. Part-time courses, especially those which are commercially sponsored, could assist in meeting these objectives, though there is a danger that such courses will be based upon an uncritical, narrow vocationalism. Such an approach could also be detrimental to those social science and humanities part-time courses that are so popular with mature students.

A much larger group, whose views are articulated by Baroness Warnock and Eli Kidourie, oppose the undermining of academic authority by market forces (Warnock 1989; Kidourie 1989). Their views do not preclude part-time routes but they do affect what people can legitimately do, and hence who has access. Warnock sees higher education as naturally elitist:

> Univerities must remain at the top of the educational pyramid, not only in the sense that they are the last ladder rungs, chronologically, to be attained by those climbing up towards the educational heights, but also in

the crucial sense that not everyone will climb so far. There is, and must always be an intellectual elite, responsible for innovation and discovery, and the inculcation and preservation of academic standards. And it follows that *what* is provided at university must remain ultimately the responsibility of the universities themselves.

Warnock 1989

She adds to this a meritocratic element in which academic (not to be confused with social) egalitarianism comes from 'a selection procedure and a teaching system which gives equal opportunities to those who present themselves as candidates' (Warnock 1989). Thus a wider pool of potential students can be trawled but only in order to compete for a conventional university education. To open the university to all abilities would be to undermine its function.

This latter view is reflected in the arguments of many who see themselves as liberal elements in higher education. The liberal rhetoric on 'academic tenure', 'standards' and 'maintenance grants' is posed in different language but still amounts to academic control of the 'best' product, including the 'best' quality of entrants, though mysteriously drawing in greater numbers, from more diverse social and economic groups. The liberal view most sympathetic to continuing education, sees higher education as reflecting, in a mediated way, a more complex and diverse society. Here society does not grant authority to academia to be exercised like divine right. Authority is democratically negotiated. This occurs more frequently on part-time courses taking non-standard students, where the authority of the lecturer and the discipline have to be established through a process of negotiation. Opening up higher education means much more than extending access to more or less the same education. It involves making higher education part of social life, in a sense, secularizing it, so that it is used and supported by the society in which it resides. The continuing education perspective, in denying the English university as the only available model for a potentially expanded system, raises serious questions of pedagogy.

A rationale may be embraced to a different degree between faculties and departments, though, as the Training Agency has noted (Fulton and Ellwood 1989), there is a tendency towards an institutional profile which, especially in the universities, typically reflects a deep-rooted conservatism towards students who do not match traditional entry requirements. A survey conducted by the Universities Council for Adult and Continuing Education concluded that, for part-time students, universities operated a 'bewildering *ad hoc* non system' of admissions (Universities Council for Adult and Continuing Education 1990). While the Department of Education and Science may set the administrative boundaries of higher education, the academic status of new arrangements will be set by those who control the system internally. It would take a dramatic fall in demand, coupled with more stringent financial measures, to force a serious rethink in terms of continuing education in institutions and departments that find no difficulty in recruiting conventional students.

The importance of the new stage approach lies in its attempt to reassess the principles and practices that have developed since the reforms of the 1960s. It acknowledges the significance of the conventional model of provision while drawing attention to its coexistence, within many institutions in both sectors, with the continuing educational model. It also looks to the factors which accentuate differences, polarizing continuing and conventional education as irreconcilable opposites. The new stage sees the erosion of the binary divide as providing the conditions for a reshaped system based on a new rationale. The move of the polytechnics and non-voluntary colleges out of local authority control, the increase in postgraduate and research work and the attempt by many polytechnics to become universities, has blurred the *raison d'être* that distinguishes them from universities. The universities, which have stressed quality and excellence in contrast to the populist rationale of extending opportunity, have had to rethink their objectives in the light of financial constraints and modifications to academic freedom. In spite of the perpetuation of the binary divide some convergence is evolving, which offers the possibility of access being widened while upholding 'standards' and advancing knowledge.

Two possibilities for part-time provision emerge from this process of convergence. One is that the universities will become more open to part-time students, like their polytechnic counterparts. The other can be seen in the trend towards national central control, coupled with managerialism at the local operational level (Lockwood 1987; Jones and Killoh 1987). Given government commitment to increasing part-time provision this centralizing tendency could assist in the development and implementation of a more universal and consistent policy towards part-time provision.

The knowledge dimension

Contemporary challenges to the ownership of higher education face a conservative, though by no means homogeneous, culture. New stake holders, and those embracing the continuing education perspective, who attempt to effect changes in established academic practices, will require the cooperation of what Becher (1989) calls the 'academic tribes'. Excellence and quality, core values of higher education and the cornerstone of academic freedom, are grounded in the guardianship and development of knowledge. Institutions of higher education are repositories of knowledge and act as intergenerational transmitters of what is considered to be worth knowing. What counts as knowledge, its classification and distribution is decided by academic 'gatekeepers'. From the sum total of culture aspects are selected, classified and organized into disciplines, subdivided into subjects and packaged as courses and curricula. To assess the effect of this on part-time higher education, the organization of knowledge is approached from what we will term the 'provider' perspective and the 'new stage' perspective.

The provider perspective

Knowledge is frequently discussed in terms of contrasts. It can be pure or applied, vocational or liberal, specialist or generalist, practical or theoretical. A dominant view, labelled the 'logic of knowledge', regards knowledge as preconstructed and free of personal or social influences (Hirst 1965; Hirst and Peters 1970). One consequence of this is that the forms of organization and transmission of knowledge appear to be determined by the inherent properties of knowledge. Academic arrangements appear as given and necessary, not the result of professional strategies and social conventions. Academic disciplines develop a life of their own with hierarchical forms of organization based on the hierarchy of knowledge. Selecting knowledge for a course, examining and grading it, is a major factor in the power and control of academics. The acquisition of, and progress in, knowledge occurs in specified time scales determined by the complexity inherent in the knowledge itself. The high priests of knowledge test the acolytes in appropriate ways in their advancement towards a mastery of the corpus of knowledge. The acolytes are graded as to their achievement relative to each other according to standards given in the knowledge. Many academic practices stem from, and are justified by, the primacy of 'true', 'pure' or 'objective' knowledge, thereby placing a closure on the possibility of alternatives and democratic challenges to outcomes.

Even those who adopt alternative views accept that the control of knowledge is a strong support for provider control. Squires (1990), examining the functions of the curriculum of higher education, has stressed the dominance of the subject in the organization of the system. The course has been a central feature of higher education, acting as the basis of staff development, student participation and administrative structures. Discussions about learning and student need are often expressed in terms of course arrangements.

There are two implications for continuing and part-time education stemming from academic control and the logic of knowledge. The first relates to the relationship of the learner to the provider. This view of knowledge does not preclude part-time routes or adult education. In fact Patterson (1984) and Lawson (1982) both maintain that adult education should initiate students into discipline based bodies of knowledge. Similarly, many part-time degrees, which are extensions of full-time or free standing honours, adopt this pedagogy. A major criticism of this is provided by Jarvis (1985), who sees much adult, vocational and distance education as education from above. The selection of educational knowledge, and the methods used, are directed by the providers and emphasize teaching rather than learning. Jarvis (1981) also draws our attention to the fact that most part-time distance learning consists of the learner being assessed through conventional examinations in preselected and packaged knowledge.

The other implication relates to the tendency for institutions to concentrate upon the capabilities of their initial entrants, especially those which correspond or fit with education from above. This extension of school is concerned more with the process of entry and progress through courses than with the diversity of outcomes. In so doing it has been successful in the production of an educational elite. Part-time degree courses have to some extent extended access to this elite. Entrance is obtained through equivalent professional or vocational certification, or through open entry. However, progress and success have often been judged on the capacity of students to adapt to education from above.

The new stage perspective

This perspective draws upon the control version of educational knowledge. Control does not deny logical knowledge but disagrees that its organization and distribution are determined by its intrinsic nature. It addresses the social factors and practices which influence the production of different knowledge based activities, as well as how categories like science, humanities, and even curricula subjects, become demarcated from each other. The control view of educational knowledge accepts that there are different forms of knowledge, which to varying degrees are influenced by society, and that in the learning process these knowledges are open to personal construction.

In one version of the control perspective the determination of ideas and thought is grounded in the social division of labour (Young 1971; Giroux 1983). Here knowledge not only divides and subdivides into specialisms but reflects, in terms of status, the hierarchical features of that social division, especially of the gradings within and between mental and manual labour. Issues of the validity of logical knowledge are of less importance than how knowledge is distributed and transmitted. Access to different types of knowledge, their organization and the different meanings generated in teaching and learning are central, as are the outcomes of the process. The application of this to the learning process means that students are seen as bearers of different types of knowledge, from which, if we accept the relevance of what the student offers, a variety of meanings and understandings emerge.

Recognition, both of the limitations of a producer-led system and of the importance of the needs of the learner, underpins the new stage perspective on access and learning. Under the banner of 'more means different' and 'fitness for purpose' the debate has shifted from an emphasis on the need to transmit content and attitudes appropriate for employers to one which locates the requirements of the active, self-directed learner at the centre of higher education. This fits well with the strong version of continuing education.

A more user-led education based on a learning relationship between equals rather than from above, and in which outcomes are evaluated on a value-added basis, opens up possibilities for wider access through more flexible forms of organization. These range from learning contracts (Knowles 1978), and self-directed learning facilitated by institutions, to attendance on a variety of part-time modes.

The time dimension

This dimension relates to the other dimensions in a very direct way since decisions about the allocation and use of time produce a variety of educational experiences. The organization and allocation of time gives considerable academic control over the enterprise of learning and the achievement of educational objectives. Different educational experiences, expressed as attainments over time, channel those participating into a number of educational routes or pathways. The drive for efficiency, following the new funding arrangements, means that many unquestioned time related activities are no longer seen as intrinsic and knowledge determined. The division of time into courses, lectures, seminars etc., and the time it takes to achieve competence, appear increasingly as social conventions rather than as intrinsic to learning.

The development of joint programmes with European institutions, and the mobility of skilled labour, has opened up the issues of commensurate qualifications and the organization of different national systems of higher education. The privileges granted to the full-time student are less prevalent on the continent. This comparative aspect, which is likely to grow in significance after 1992, adds to the debate about the length and time structure of different courses. Academic conventions involving these time factors, which are incorporated in the conditions of service of academics, are geared to full-time students. Those who can only attend in the evening as part-time students are often bemused by the distribution of educational resources based on full-time staff and students operating on a timetable similar to schools over a 30 to 36 week year!

The demand for more effective measures of performance and the spread of modularization both require a review of what actually goes on, or is learned in, these portions of academic time. In spite of the work of the CNAA and HMIs to establish comparative standards it is far from clear to staff or students what the most effective use of time is. Moreover, comparable qualifications within or between disciplines and institutions have different time structures. This is hardly surprising when we consider the anomalies in the length of a supposed standard unit: is it, for example, a tutorial, term or academic year (each of which differ between sectors and institutions)? Proposals for credit accumulation and transfer schemes have emphasized differences in workloads between subjects, though institutions are not usually prepared to discuss the findings in public.

Attending, quantitatively, for nine (or twelve) ten week terms, over three or four academic years, tells us little qualitatively about the effective use of that time or the standard of education offered. With an increasing number of students working to support themselves, and the proposed changes to the benefit system likely to force many more to do so, the line between full-time and part-time study is beginning to blur. Part-time degrees that involve something more than the extension of a full-time programme, especially those that are free standing, challenge the assumptions and practices of full-time study.

Temporal features in schooling and participation in higher education

As educational routes, part-time higher education courses are part of the structure of the wider educational system and they are connected to a channelling process operating at different levels of that system. The education system is composed of a number of networks which operate to process inputs at one level of the system into outputs. Some of these outputs become inputs to another level or stage in the system. The entry, exit and internal transfer points are based on time factors that are decided administratively.

Higher education requires schooling to develop the intellectual capacities which it presupposes to exist in its prospective students, and through selective and filtering mechanisms supply it with a sufficient quantity and quality of inputs. While higher education is dependent on the size and quality of school outputs it exerts considerable downward pressure on the system. To maintain standards access must be policed predominantly through competitive examinations. The selective 'A' level is still the passport to higher education. Here the age of 18 has been significant for entry to, and 21 for exit from, higher education. From the perspective of continuing education this process has produced a mass of citizens whose choices and horizons have been structured and limited; who neither qualify nor perceive themselves as suitable for higher education. One function of the part-time course is to respond to student needs at different life stages.

Those who make the 'correct' choices in the formal system are able to enter higher education through a direct route. Others do so through entry into an occupation which requires furthering one's education. A considerable amount of part-time provision is in the area of occupationally related education and training. Many in the school system do not get as far as the occupational route: for them the age of 16 heralds the termination or winding down of their educational career. Fifty per cent of young people leave school at 16, and only 30 per cent are left at 17 (HM Senior Inspector of Schools 1989). One outcome of educational channelling is that many young people are not equipped to proceed to higher education, or to enter occupations which increasingly require an advanced education, even if subsequently they wish to do so. One remedial aspect of continuing education involves healing and compensating for the negative experiences of educational channelling.

Educational careers and part-time higher education

A useful way of assessing the temporal effects of schooling on participation in higher education is through the use of the concept of the educational career, which draws our attention to 'a course through life'. Its sociological usage connects subjective and group experiences to occupational, institutional and social structures. Within the compulsory system children are involved in a process of selection and allocation. Decisions are made on progress and the children themselves make choices, though not under conditions necessarily of their own choosing. The concept of educational career, when applied to the educational advancement of an individual or group through an organizational network, would take account of external factors such as class, environment, ethnicity and gender which might affect progress (Purvis and Hales 1983; Willis 1977).

Those involved in the planning and teaching of part-time programmes need to understand the complex profile of subjective meanings and material outcomes of the previous educational experiences of their students. It is essential for those promoting wider access to understand the relevant aspects of the educational career of those they wish to encourage to enter higher education, and the progress made once a route has been selected (Smith and Saunders 1988). The new stage perspective requires that we adopt new ways of assessing these experiences, both for adequate communication and in order to measure the value-added.

The part-time student differs from the traditional full-time student, whose educational career often corresponds to the expectations of higher education or who at least has had time to adjust to them. The work–study relationship, particularly in the area of the allocation of time, affects the socialization of part-time students into the institution, and their progress. It can lead to a demand for different types of teaching and assessment. Incomprehension and conflict can arise from a failure to integrate different educational careers into the pedagogy and expectations of the institutions.

Detailed student profiles based upon occupation and lifestyles can assist us in re-establishing educational careers in part-time and continuing education. In doing so we are moving away from the course as conventionally conceived and towards the educational career as the basis for promoting learning. Relevant factors here include age and occupational stage, the timing of provision, and of the achievement of learning objectives. A restructuring of resources may be required, as well as additional resources and different skills from those normally used with conventional students.

The attempt to establish a national curriculum and alter the system of examinations is likely to produce changes in higher education from below. The recognition of underachievement and the pattern of educational careers, noted above, coupled with the state's desire to increase participation, raises some vital issues for continuing education, especially regarding the role of part-time degrees. Part-time degrees are for those who chose vocational routes which deferred higher education until later in the lifecycle. Such students demand a degree of occupational relevance that can assist occupational mobility. However, increasing access need not be through part-time routes. More students could be processed through the conventional mode and the typical educational career could be restructured accordingly. For example, funding could be directed towards keeping 16–19-year-olds on at school or college rather than increasing the numbers of mature part-time students. This solution fits closely with the conventional perspective of more of the same. Those embracing the broad version of the continuing education perspective, while not wishing to deprive such students, would, however, wish to see restructuring as part of a larger process of widening access so that higher education internally became more comprehensive and diverse.

Extending educational careers

Any move towards widening access and embracing a more developed model of continuing education has to acknowledge those lifecycle implications which connect the organization and resourcing of higher education to educational careers. Delayed participation is the most common form of continuing education. This may simply mean deferring entry until after the cônventional entry point at 18. It is worth noting that the Department of Education and Science has recently introduced into its projections a Younger Mature Entry Index for potential entrants aged 21–24 (Department of Education and Science 1986b). This recognizes the issue of deferred choice and suggests that it is expected to become more common. This is indicative of the impact of the demographic downturn in producing effects not only on potential student numbers but also on the labour markets for young people. A scarcity factor is arising, so that there is competition for

> able, young people between commercial concerns and higher education. There has been a concentration on the disparity between projected graduate demand and the supply, with fears of an overall deficit and acute shortages in particular areas . . .
>
> Pearson and Pike 1989a

The Treasury, in the debates about student loans, has noted the problems that arise for employers when there are skill shortages resulting from reduced numbers of educated 18-year-olds, some of whom prefer to enter higher education. The effect of these disparities has been to increase the starting salaries of this group. Eighteen-year-olds with 'A' levels, or 16-year-olds about to enter the sixth form, may prefer to enter well paid jobs, though this does not preclude their wishing to enter higher education at a later stage in their careers.

Here is a golden opportunity for part-time provision to design courses for the interests and abilities of such late entrants, while still permitting them to progress in their chosen occupation, or perhaps, to switch occupations. However, a note of caution must be exercised, for the rate of growth of part-time higher education must not lead us to assume that all that matters is a willingness to undertake a course. Another time factor, in respect of employment, enters here. Coldstream, from the employers' perspective, has advocated the negotiation of a right to education as part of the labour contract, at least for highly skilled workers (Coldstream 1989). Thus, employers are encouraged to solve short-term labour shortages by offering time incentives later on and the young are encouraged to accept the inconveniences of subsequent part-time study for the benefit of an immediate and attractive salary. Those electing to do this will have to face a problem common to many part-time students. One source of non-completion, even by well motivated students who are allowed time off for study by their employers, is that the tasks which comprise their jobs are goal, not time, specific. Unlike time-oriented jobs, where the definition of the job consists of what you do between certain hours, those in occupations where tasks are seemingly never completed can find demands made upon them which prevent them studying or attending even when allowed release.

The recurrent education approach extends further the notion that education is a lifelong activity. In essence it means that for periods throughout their working lives individuals may return to education. The key difficulty here is one of cost, both to the employer and to the individual and his/her dependants. A system of sabbaticals can operate either in the form of paid leave or through an educational voucher, granted by the state for the full cost. This can involve a mix of private and public funding. Rehn (1972), reporting to the Organization for Economic Co-operation and Development, proposed an educational fund integrated into social insurance schemes. As with sickness benefit and pensions this fund could be drawn upon at a particular point.

Embling (1974) has developed this to look at work/non-work patterns and emphasizes individuals' ability to mix a proportion of entitlements to leisure, education and pension. There is a sense in which such a scheme would operate like a loan scheme, with students commuting future insurance payments to pay for current education. There are, of course, several disadvantages. Employers might have difficulties planning production and could lose skilled labour at strategic times. The 'live now pay later' element might affect old age where a sickness arises and individuals might opt for leisure as opposed to socially and economically desirable education. However, the advantages of choice and access would ameliorate the negative effects if part-time provision could be built into such schemes. Part-time education, by providing flexibility, could reduce the high cost of maintenance and alleviate the loss of key workers, while still allowing them to exercise their entitlements when they chose to do so.

In concentrating on economic implications we must not forget two important factors. The first is relevant to the student voucher schemes being considered by Training and Enterprise Councils. Like the American Private Industry Councils' scheme, vouchers may empower potential students to choose education or training. Conversely, without good independent support and counselling it might permit employers to dictate their own training needs at the expense of student interest. Less materialistically, there is an important sector of further and higher education which is undertaken on a voluntary and self-directed basis (Department of Education and Science 1987b; Jarvis 1989). The willingness of considerable numbers of people to enter adult education and mainly non-vocational courses, is evidence that demand is not merely instrumental and that provision needs to reflect this by emphasizing its educational value as well as the attractiveness of its financial packages.

The method dimension

The third dimension making up the educational mode of organization is that of method. Method can be defined both in terms of delivery technologies and in terms of administrative structures. In the final chapter we will look at some of the technologies, like distance learning and credit accumulation and transfer, involved in continuing education. In this chapter we will limit ourselves to looking at administrative structures. Our treatment of this dimension differs from that of the others in that we make use of data detailing the practices observed in our panel study of institutions.

Organizational types

Part-time higher education is not a single entity. As we demonstrated in Chapter 3, it is offered in the daytime, in the evening or as a mix of both. It may take the form of a free standing degree, or as an addition to existing full-time provision. The aim can be to attract individuals or it may be devised in relation to employers' (public or private sector) needs. This diversity of provision has understandably led to variety in organization. There appear to be three ideal typical ways of organizing part-time provision within the institutions which we observed. We call these the departmental model, the independent degree model and the centralizing tendency.

The departmental model
Most part-time degrees remain the responsibility of subject departments. Within the department part-time provision is generally the responsibility of a part-time tutor or coordinator who is, in effect, the course head. This model has certain financial advantages in protecting expensive part-time provision (Chapter 4), but these must be balanced against the tendency for degrees to have low status within departments, for the course tutor to lack authority, especially in the allocation of staff, and the difficulty in expanding or even controlling part-time recruitment. A further difficulty for institutions where part-time programmes are departmentalized lies in ensuring coherence of provision across departments, and particularly in offering interdisciplinary courses. In short, provision tends to be patchy and future planning often lacks coherence. Under departmental organization, provision can be free standing or additional, though where it is free standing the course tutor's freedom of action is normally constrained.

The independent degree model
Organizational independence has been achieved by some part-time degrees in circumstances particular to the institution in which they reside. This independence has obvious advantages in terms of the recognition and response to patterns of demand and direct control of recruitment. It is usually associated with a high staff commitment to part-time education (at least among those

teaching on the degree) and this may well be reflected in the quality of provision, especially in terms of the quality of contact with students. However, such provision tends to be relatively expensive, and perhaps more importantly, is more likely to be perceived to be more expensive. Single subject courses and/or those with relatively low levels of recruitment are often rather vulnerable, both to fluctuations in student demand, and to cost cutting exercises within the institution.

In some respects university extramural departments might be seen to be included within this model. They differ in that they do not typically offer high status (i.e. degree level) work and must seek staff and support from other departments which often see such activity as peripheral. A recent development is the independent cross-departmental part-time degree programme, with its own independent head and ancillary administrative staff. This interesting development eradicates most of the disadvantages of the independent degree. By giving the part-time degree quasi-departmental status, with its own course office or registry, and with a clear budget, its status and political muscle within the institution is substantially improved. However, such provision tends to be expensive and most receive some explicit or implicit subsidy from institutional funds. This means that such programmes are vulnerable until such time as there is a more realistic match between funding and the calculated costs of provision. It should also be stressed that, while in a few cases such programmes offer enormous breadth of provision, they typically do not extend across the institution's total range of provision or even include all of the part-time programmes.

The centralizing tendency

Another recent development intended to raise the profile of part-time provision has been the appointment of a coordinator or controller of part-time education. This may be combined with departmental status, with the head of part-time programme coordinating areas of institutional provision. A number of institutions have attempted to give coherence to their part-time, associate student and short course provision, irrespective of the type of degrees they run, by appointing a senior coordinator.

Some discussion of administrative terminology is appropriate at this point. Although some of these academic administrative positions predate public debate over finance and numbers in higher education, they have arisen from the same external pressure to increase the emphasis both upon part-time and mature students. However, the term continuing education is used quite differently in different institutions. Thus the head of continuing education in one institution might restrict his/her brief to part-time students, whereas in another he/she might have responsibility additionally for mature full-time students and intensive short courses. To the extent that institutions are under pressure to accommodate more of both, there are certain advantages to the latter definition. On the other hand, the interests of part-time students and full-time mature students may not be the same and indeed may well conflict over the allocation of diminishing resources.

Such difficulties aside, there are many claimed advantages to centralizing the control of part-time provision in the form of a head of part-time education, especially where that head is supported by a separate registry or administrative unit. It may lead to greater efficiency of operation in reducing the duplication of student services and in seeking to rationalize course provision. It may also be more effective in coordinating future part-time initiatives. It offers a focus for the resources which can now be geared specifically to part-time provision. It may increase the political weight of the interests within the institution in terms of bids for additional resources, academic provision other than teaching – as in library loan systems and the opening hours of catering facilities for part-time students – and in terms of improving the conditions of life for part-timers. Additionally it can provide a high profile externally, allowing, for example, the provision of part-time advertising budgets, 'high street' access points in shop front locations and a clear point of contact for admissions and for the resolution of specifically part-time problems. The possibility of transcending factional interests allows a more flexible response to changing markets.

While the tendency to centralize the organization of part-time provision can have all of the above advantages, it also has a number of serious problems associated with it. Taken out of academic hands, there is a tendency for the curriculum to become eclectic, with the creation of large general or combined studies degrees, lacking the coherence of subject – or problem-oriented courses. This could lead to a failure to understand the differing academic needs of students wishing to study different disciplines or with different vocational interests. Thus general science or general arts degrees may militate against producing competent physicists or competent historians – from a discipline perspective – or competent managers or competent engineers – in terms of vocational requirements. This is not to say that 'linear' or vocationally specific degrees cannot operate within such programmes. It is rather that many academics feel that overcentralization of course organization leads to communication problems in terms of the transmission of their professional concerns into the system.

A further danger which can arise from the centralizing tendency lies in the nature of the functions required of a co-ordinator and the possible conflicts which may arise. The coordinator may have any combination of three functions to perform: to coordinate the operation of the programme; to act in a public relations role for the programme; and to act as an entrepreneur seeking external finance for specific programmes or courses. All of the functions may be more efficiently and effectively conducted if they are separated. However, the extent of the centralizing tendency should not be exaggerated. Of the institutions which we visited only half had made significant moves towards either cross-faculty independent degree programmes or the appointment of part-time or continuing education coordinators.

Organizational types and the part-time student

Organizational types of part-time provision are varied precisely because they have arisen in response to local demand, and to initiatives developed internally. The range of detailed variations in practice has been catalogued by Barnett (Barnett 1986). While some of these undoubtedly represent bad as well as good practice, they have arisen in relation to particular local demands and conditions. Given the variable demands for part-time higher education (Tight 1982), it is not surprising to find wide variations in institutional response.

The public relations, entrepreneurial and administrative functions of centralization all relate to the business model of education. Each, in itself, is perfectly laudable to the extent that it brings real organizational benefits to continuing and part-time education. In terms of the range of provision and number of places there is no doubt that gains have been made. Since these factors might act as a model for future developments we will explore in detail some of the problems arising with them in part-time provision.

Marketing part-time degrees

In business products are marketed by marketing specialists. Some of the consequences of allowing academics to market their own wares have been revealed by Barnett's survey of part-time degree practices (Barnett 1986). He found the literature to be badly produced and unattractively presented. Information was at times incoherent, with apparently irrelevant application forms and inadequate arrangements for enrolment and induction. Some of this arises from lack of awareness or lack of skills on the part of academics, though as Barnett himself acknowledges it also relates to lack of institutional resources both in manpower and money. There is no doubt that centralizing the marketing of part-time programmes can produce substantial improvements in the quality of presentation by creating skilled manpower and by providing a location for the allocation of part-time budgets. A centralized advertising budget for part-time provision, for example, allows for the possibility of new kinds of advertising. Some institutions are now using television advertising – an opportunity not normally available to individual part-time degrees. Others have used a centralized part-time registry not just to administrate part-time provision but to offer an advisory service for potential students.

All of these are real benefits but they must be set against potential problems. It should be remembered that the part-time student population is not homogeneous. Demand differs along at least three dimensions (see above). Our observations of actual institutional practice led us to believe that centralizing the organization of part-time provision seems to be most effective in attracting individual students rather than organizational ones, in attracting generalists rather than those seeking specialist courses and in attracting students on to daytime rather than evening courses, though a number of institutions in established areas of provision are now offering evening only programmes which are centrally organized. In the latter case they do successfully recruit to evening courses but this is rarely accompanied by daytime provision for part-time students. Demand for specialist degrees and diplomas appears to relate more to specialist departments. Where institutions have stressed growth this has tended to be in terms of generalist, individual daytime demand.

Seeking new markets and responding to them
It is agreed by advocates of the centralizing tendency that the greater efficiency, coherence and resources obtained encourage greater responsiveness to demand. We found examples of individual part-time degrees with very low recruitment figures desperately seeking to maintain demand for their course out of departmental interest. It could be argued that resources might be better utilized elsewhere. Where new patterns of demand emerge a central organization can more rapidly respond, overreaching as it does departmental pressures for the status quo. The difficulty facing central organizations lies precisely in their capacity to recognize or create new demands. As we argued above, a central part-time registry is often very effective in picking up new forms of individual demand and in directing potential demand into current course provision. However, organizational (employer) demand tends to operate differently. While some professions have themselves identified a new need for graduate status, or externally assessed professionally oriented courses, and have actively sought an academic location for their ambitions, most employer demand for higher education has tended to come from lengthy, detailed, specialist negotiations about the form and content of provision. Centralized registries tend to lack these specialist skills and the knowledge required to identify potential demand. Such negotiations are also expensive. Therefore, despite what may be very substantial benefits from such arrangements both financially (Chapter 4) and educationally (Tight 1987), stimulating individual demand is often more attractive in the short term.

Such an argument would not be so serious were it not for the emphasis of the government and its agencies upon the importance of employer demand. It would be ironic in the extreme if those forward thinking institutions which have tried to anticipate future trends should find themselves with an organization directed at the 'wrong' recruitment strategy.

Efficient administration
The third major argument for the centralizing tendency is that it facilitates the efficient administration of part-time provision through the concentration of a specialist administration and economies of scale. The advantages which it can serve in terms of coherent and efficient administration are obvious and need not be detailed. However, once again, we wish to balance this, not just with warnings about the dangers of over-bureaucratized centralism but also with the danger of competing aims. One institution we examined exemplified the problem in almost every facet. This institution had successfully developed an effective central administration for part-time provision. It claimed success in improving recruitment rates not only to degree programmes but also to rapidly

expanding associate student/short course programmes. The focus of the central part-time administration was exclusively on individual demand, linked with a commitment to freedom of student choice within increasingly individualized programmes. However, academic staff running and teaching actual academic programmes dismissed in disparaging terms this 'supermarket' approach to higher education. Their emphasis was upon the identification of professional groups, industrial concerns and specific firms as sources of demand which could be channelled into integrated academic programmes with little student choice.

In the absence of a stated educational philosophy mediating each level of practice there are serious disadvantages to the centralizing tendency. Overcentralization and bureaucratization can produce an incoherence in the operation of the different levels of institutional activity, and so undermine the operation of each level. Indeed, the issue here goes beyond that of coherence. The principles involved mirror current conflicts, especially in the PCFC sector, concerning the balance between the executive and democratic dimensions of managerial authority and control and the market or academic orientation of the institutions. The centralizing tendency represents a move towards and an emphasis upon executive action and market orientation and away from the more traditional – particularly in the universities – emphasis upon democratic (collegiate) action and academic orientation. The need to respond to a new market situation may not be incompatible with academic and collegiate concerns but we must recognize that developing organizational structures in response to immediate concerns may not act in the long term interest of the institutions.

Conclusions

We have noted a number of organizational structures operating in part-time higher education. These range from departmental models of provision to the existence of independent degrees. Two particular trends have been discerned from the recent substantial increase in part-time student numbers: the introduction of cross-faculty, independent degree provision and the centralizing tendency. We have discussed the advantages and disadvantages of these various organization models as effective structures and have attempted to relate these to wider concerns of educational philosophy.

The centralizing tendency has much to recommend it in terms of providing an organizational coherence and positive image. It can also channel resources into part-time education and respond to a variety of student demands as well as seeking out new markets. We also detect a move to an intermediate position between centralization and the departmental or independent degree model. This consists of the appointment of part-time (or continuing education) coordinators within each faculty or cost centre. It is said to increase the coherence and effectiveness of provision within each faculty while ensuring a proper sympathetic relationship to academic concerns and a clear relationship between executive and democratic dimensions. Its effectiveness is as yet untested. Its danger, of course, lies in interfaculty rivalry which may lead to less coherence at the wider institutional level.

6 | Continuing Debates and Future Prospects

We began this book by acknowledging the commonplace of rapid social change in higher education. We have attempted to incorporate the main features of the contemporary debate within our core analysis. However, the speed and range of change is such that new issues are constantly arising. In this chapter we will review in more detail some contemporary developments and their implications for part-time provision. First we consider the implications of the decision to maintain the binary divide between the university and the polytechnic and college sectors. Then we look at a range of initiatives which are affecting part-time provision.

The effects of the new funding bodies

The White Paper introduced by Kenneth Baker in early 1987 shifted the emphasis of higher education. It acknowledged that '[T]he encouragement of a high level of scholarship in the arts, humanities and social sciences is an essential feature of a civilised and cultured country' and that '[M]eeting the needs of the economy is not the sole purpose of higher education . . . But this aim, with its implications for the scale and quality of higher education, must be vigorously pursued' (Department of Education and Science 1987a). The 'needs of the economy' are somewhat narrowly defined in the White Paper which aims to shift the balance of courses towards science and engineering, and business and management studies. This somewhat kneejerk response may well not be the most effective way of meeting the needs of the economy.

The White Paper also takes access seriously. While modifying the Robbins principle of access to all who are suitably qualified, it also 'invites all those with relevant responsibilities to consider carefully the steps necessary to secure increased participation by both young and *older people*' [our emphasis] and act accordingly. Yet it fails to recognize the anomaly that non-standard entry and part-time degree programmes have been particularly popular in what have been designated 'non-favoured areas': i.e. humanities and social sciences. This has been reflected subsequently in the underrecruitment of courses in engineering despite the best efforts of UGC and particularly NAB to expand in this area, and in the PCFC's decision to reduce the number of subject areas in order to lump together non-favoured areas of provision.

Subsequent legislation has paved the way for the establishment of two new funding bodies and the independence of what was previously the public sector from local authority control. There was much pressure from the Committee of Directors of Polytechnics for the establishment of a single funding body to cover both the universities and the newly independent polytechnics and colleges of higher education. This was rejected in favour of two separate bodies: the Universities Funding Council (UFC) and the Polytechnics and Colleges Funding Council (PCFC), so that 'for the first time Britain will have two parallel *national* systems of higher education' (*Times Higher Educational Supplement* 1988).

The membership of both new bodies certainly suggests that the original intention was that they should remain separate in the forseeable future, for, their memberships imply quite different functions. The UFC membership very much reflects continuity with the UGC it replaces, specifically excluding vice-chancellors and other heads of institutions which it funds, whereas the new PCFC membership 'has a more managerial and even representative feel than the UFC' (*Times Higher Educational Supplement* 1988), is smaller than the NAB was and lacks its formal intelligence gathering links with HM Inspectors and with the CNAA. Whether this separation will now continue in the longer term is coming increasingly into doubt. The main difference between UGC and NAB funding levels had been the research element built into the former – indeed this had been a major source of contention for the polytechnics (Rickett 1987). If the universities lose their research base and become 'teaching institutions' why should their funding levels differ from those of the other sector, especially when many polytechnics have successfully attracted external funding in order to run substantial research programmes? In September 1989 the UFC conducted its own research selectivity exercise. While it was careful to rate subject areas rather than institutions as a whole, it is not difficult to identify those institutions which have a low score across the board. No doubt the universities will seek alternative rationales to justify the differential level of funding if this element disappears. Nevertheless, the present government has shown some signs of acknowledging that the research base is a more appropriate basis for 'elite' funding, and presumably 'elite' status, than the designation university or polytechnic.

The issue is an important one for continuing education, and particularly for part-time higher education, because so much of this is located in the polytechnics and colleges of higher education. The UGC never publicly revealed the level of the research element in its funding, preferring to offer each institution a block grant to cover both research and teaching commitments. Once the research element is separated out from the grant for teaching any discrepancy between sector costs would be more difficult to justify. Indeed, if we acknowledge the legitimacy of a value-added model of funding as advocated by Robinson (1988), there is a strong case for arguing for additional funding to the polytechnic sector to the extent that it serves mature, non-standard entrants. In the case of part-time students the case is even stronger for, even ignoring the differences in the unit of resource, the PCFC sector receives a lower FTES rate per part-time student than do the universities.

The major organizational impact of the new funding bodies will undoubtedly fall upon the polytechnic and college sector, which now is constituted as a national system of higher education. We can only guess at the precise consequences of this for continuing and part-time education. Some, like Robinson, fear the loss of the local connection. Certainly the PCFC may, if it chooses, have a much more direct impact upon either type of provision. The position outlined so far suggests that the planning model will be an open one (Dearing 1988). It will very much depend upon how contractual arrangements develop (National Association of Teachers in Further and Higher Education 1988). We can but hope that the PCFC's decision to separate the categories of part-time, full-time and sandwich students will be used positively to encourage part-time provision. The Polytechnic Association for Continuing Education (PACE) have argued that performance indicators for institutions must include reference to their continuing education provision. If the government is really serious about expanding non-standard mature entry it may even be feasible to pose contracts specifically in terms of this type of student. The PCFC's (and UFC's) reference to 'quality' and 'quantity', do little to enlighten us. Eighteen-year-olds tend to be better qualified and cheaper to teach from the institutions' point of view. If they get priority in 'elite' institutions we may well find that those who specialize in the more time consuming, less well qualified students will also be required to operate on criteria of quantity and so receive less funding proportionately.

The PCFC Consultative Document on Funding Choices (PCFC 1989) is both encouraging and discouraging for continuing and part-time education. It notes 'wider access' first in its list of pressures on the higher education system and it highlights the Secretary of State's objective to the PCFC

> to increase participation among all types of student, including women, ethnic minorities, those with a wider range of academic and practical experience than before, and those without traditional entry requirements.
>
> PCFC 1989a

However it makes no reference to part-time students whatsoever. The emphasis of the document is very firmly upon the importance of student demand: '*well-informed student demand could and should play the major role in deciding how funds should be distributed* [our emphasis], although it should not be the sole determinant' (PCFC 1989a). This market model rather depends on supplying an existing demand. However the expansion of education to the 'minority' groups mentioned above is to a degree untested demand. The situation for part-time provision is even worse. Demand studies are expensive and therefore rare, and we know from past experience that where part-time education is offered it tends to be taken up but that evidence of demand prior to take up is difficult to demonstrate (Robinson 1988).

The new organizational arrangements will have another consequence for continuing education in so far as they have an impact upon access arrangements. For the first time in the public sector, there will be a separation between higher education degree level provision and further education. In fact polytechnic-type institutions will still be able to offer further education courses and not all institutions offering higher education will become independent. However since the Act removes from the local educational authority (LEA) the duty to secure higher education provision within its area (UDACE 1988a), it seems likely that degree level courses still under LEA control will gradually wither away. It is argued that the new Act strengthens the duty of LEAs to 'secure provision of adequate Further Education' (UDACE 1988a). The danger, however, lies in the separation of continuing higher education in its full and part-time modes from the many further education access courses which feed it.

> There is a basic contradiction between improving access between FE and HE and removing most of the major HE institutions from local authority control . . . FE institutions have had to struggle hard to persuade HE to become responsive on the access issue. There is no guarantee that the new corporate, highly competitive HE institutions will become, or continue to be, responsive.

> National Association of Teachers in Further and Higher Education 1988

The rapid development of consortia has been one response to this situation. By making formal links between a range of higher education and further education institutions irrespective of their funding bases, continuity and coherence of progression can be achieved. Nevertheless, some residual concern must be expressed about the flexibility of the new arrangements and their ability to draw greater numbers of mature entrants into the formal post-school educational system and so onto degree programmes. As Figure 6.1 shows, while the majority of further education students are engaged in planned learning programmes, most are not on formal courses and only a small minority are on formal certified courses. Every effort must be made to ensure that those drawn into further education are offered opportunities to develop a formal certified education and so are given the chance to move into higher education. Credit accumulation and transfer (CATS) schemes can make a major contribution to this (see below).

Some initiatives in higher education

Credit accumulation and transfer schemes

The introduction and implementation of CATS has been a major development which has considerable implications for continuing education. The forces impelling such development have been largely economic, both in the narrow sense of saving money and in the broader sense of expanding the market for

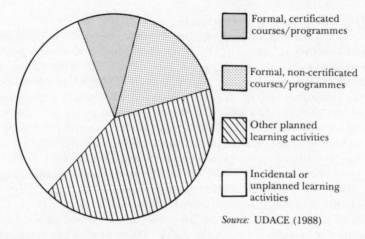

Formal, certificated
courses/programmes

Formal, non-certificated
courses/programmes

Other planned
learning activities

Incidental or
unplanned learning
activities

Source: UDACE (1988)

Figure 6.1 Learning routes in further education.

higher education into previously underexploited socio-economic groups. Although, perhaps primarily, addressing the issue of full-time students, pulling in continuing education students into institutions in the context of an assumed decline in the traditional market, it has also been a significant development for part-time students, in that the same forces which have driven higher education institutions into the education and training market place have also made them recognize their role as resource centres for the local community and economy (Portwood 1988).

The rise of CATS is closely linked with the modularization process but the two are not identical. Modularization merely divides courses into identifiable units and defines necessary combinations of units which go to make up different levels of qualifications. While modularization implies an identifiable weighting of units *within a programme* and therefore the accumulation of credit, CATS are designed specifically to allow an accumulation of credit which enables the possibility of *transfer* either between programmes within an institution or between institutions. So, for example, GCSE has been re-modelled on a modular basis; but it does not offer credit transfer arrangements except in the crudest terms (Schools Examinations Council 1988). In the most developed versions CATS incorporate modules both from a wide breadth of disciplines and a wide range of levels of study. They can then make a major contribution to access by crediting the work of associate students, short courses, in house retraining, updating and upgrading schemes, and they can enhance the prospects of transfer from full- to part-time modes of study and vice versa. When linked to local consortia either of similar institutions, like the South East England Consortia (Hilton 1989) or of institutions operating at different levels of study, like the Lancashire Integrated Colleges Scheme (Abramson 1988), they can revolutionize the possibilities for local access to higher education.

CATS schemes can be used very successfully with associate student schemes to enhance the possibilities of access. Portwood (1988) has usefully identified three major models of associate student provision currently in operation in terms of how they relate to CATS. Although his emphasis is upon associate students the models also illustrate the range of practice in terms of CATS. Portwood calls the models 'the marginal model', 'the intermediate model' and 'the mainstream model'. The marginal model is typically a free standing scheme, not conferring awards, with the emphasis on giving access to single learning units or modules. The intermediate model is incorporated within an academic course or programme in the mainstream of institutional provisional. This may be confined to a single course, often a combined studies degree, or it may be associated with a major cross-faculty development. Such a development allows for the accumulation of credit though the applicability and acceptability of credits may be restricted. The mainstream model is part of an *institutional* scheme of credit accumulation and transfer which allows students to negotiate programmes specifically suited to their needs while making their studies part of mainstream provision. A similar range of possibilities exist for the accreditation of in house training courses and occupational experience, though these are generally less fully developed.

CATS typically operate on a credit rating based either on the length of the course or its proportion of a named award. The former mechanism is attractive for those who are concerned to integrate short course and in house programmes into their schemes, though care must be taken in identifying the level of study. The latter mechanism is particularly attractive in that it allows the introduction of CATS with minimal disruption to the existing programmes. While it is often assumed that modularization will lead to standard credit rating of courses or multiples of a standard credit length this is not essential and we observed a wide range of practices during our research.

Neither is length of course or proportion of programme the only basis for credit rating. Roberts has produced a scheme (Roberts 1988) based on what he calls, 'curriculum activity' in which he includes not only formal educational settings but also private study and preparation on the part of the student. So his scheme is based not just on the institutional resources committed to a programme but also the 'notional' hours which a student will be expected to put into that programme. This is claimed to increase the flexibility of time allocation within programmes, with students receiving acknowledgement for a whole range of activity outside classes, and to encourage open learning and distance learning techniques. Whether such a system can be effective in practice remains to be seen; but it does open up the prospect of alternative bases for credit accumulation and transfer.

Typically CATS developments have arisen locally and in the context of local consortia arrangements. Inevitably they have approached issues in different and distinctive ways. This piecemeal approach has probably benefited the local regions for it has allowed variations appropriate to the local context. However, differing requirements, regulations and weightings of different schemes can present difficulties for students who are geographically mobile and who move prior to the completion of their academic programme. This is a particular problem for part-time students who take longer to complete degrees and who are often active in their career aspirations as well as their education and so are more likely to move jobs and locations. There is therefore a strong case for a national scheme. Derek Pollard's work with the CNAA's own CATS is particularly impressive in this respect (Pollard 1989). Indeed the CNAA scheme now seems likely to determine how the university sector will develop its CATS arrangements. It has the advantage of offering coherence to Cats nationally without being overly directive towards the local institutions concerned, which are allowed to determine the content and structure of programmes under the guidance of the CNAA's Committee for CATS.

The CNAA scheme also allows up to half of the credits which go to make up a qualification to accrue from prior learning. This means that a typical five-year part-time degree could be reduced to only two and a half years with appropriate advanced standing. It also allows for intermediate accreditation so that after 120 credits a certificate is awarded, and after 240, a diploma. Unfortunately, the specific form it has taken is not readily convertible to a typical five-year part-time degree format, though it is hoped that new intermediate award schemes will be devised which will allow part-time students to receive interim awards at the end of each year of study. This combination of locally sensitive consortia within an umbrella provided by the CNAA scheme, whatever the short-term difficulties, can offer real advantages particularly to part-time students. Pre-accreditation for work experience, accreditation of professional qualifications and access courses, and coherent related short course provision should go some considerable way to attracting many more part-time students to higher education.

Distance learning

Distance learning can in itself hardly be regarded as a new development. The Open University is firmly established in this country and is responsible for between one-fifth and one-quarter of all part-time students. Given that part-time students represent over one-third of the student population, the students of the Open University constitute nearly 10 per cent of all students of higher education (Department of Education and Science 1988a). What is more the idea of distance learning has spread widely throughout the world (Holmberg 1985). There have been a number of recent developments in this area which are likely to have a further impact both upon continuing education and, especially, part-time students.

One such development was that of the Open Tech. Conceived in 1983 by the Manpower Services Commission (MSC) and planned to be self-financing by 1987, it aimed to shake up the further and higher education sectors by offering pump priming money to develop, among other things, distance learning alternatives to traditional teaching methods. While its nomenclature is similar to that of the Open University, it was deliberately organized differently. The MSC's view that the Open University was both expensive and insufficiently aware of the needs of industry and commerce led it to reject the notion of a central free standing body planning and providing provision. Instead Open Tech courses were to be provided by existing educational institutions, industrial or commercial companies, local authorities or private training agencies. The central coordinating body would only be directive where it perceived a serious deficiency in need. What is more, Open Tech courses were to be cheap. Some course packages were designed to provide frameworks or supports for in house or college based provision. The most frequent criticism of this initiative (echoing that of the Open University), is that up front costs are high and that the MSC's parsimony under-primed the pump (Antill 1986).

Another ambitious attempt at open learning is the Open College of the Arts which was launched in November 1987 with an extended pilot project to offer 'innovative home-based learning material supported locally by tutorials in schools, colleges, polytechnics, or other centres' (Open College of the Arts undated). The format chosen – course book, guidebook, textbooks and materials, supported by regular group tutorials – is similar to Open University methods of teaching and indeed has its origins in earlier distance learning experiments (Smith 1968). The Open College of the Arts, however, intends to put greater emphasis on face to face teaching in local centres – perhaps the weakest aspect of the Open University's provision. Lord Young was quoted at its inception as aiming at 4,000 students in its first year, though subsequent reports suggest that the actual enrolments have been disappointing. One of their courses, The Art of Photography, has since been launched in conjunction with a national newspaper and a television series, with the promise to students to publish some of their project work in the newspaper (the *Guardian*, January 1989).

A most exciting development in distance learning is the proposal for an Open Polytechnic. The Open Polytechnic was first announced in April 1988 at the Association for Part-time Higher Education conference, where it was described as:

> a fifth or sixth generation distance learning institution which would draw on the pioneering work of the Open University and the wealth of expertise which has been built up both in Britain and internationally by other public and private distance education agencies.
>
> Richards 1988

Like the Open Tech proposals it rejected the Open University model, seeing itself as a consortium of institutions providing distance learning packages for use in conjunction with other teaching methods within collaborating institutions and integrating national provision through a coherent system of credit accumulation and transfer procedures. Three purposes were claimed to underlie the Open Polytechnic:

1. to identify key areas of higher educational provision;
2. to bring together programme teams to develop tutor and student resource materials from access to degree level; and

3. to produce and distribute these materials, with accompanying staff development support, and enable people in different institutions to use them
as part of their own courses.

In one sense, then, the Open Polytechnic will act as a publishing company,
commissioning materials and subsequently distributing them. However, it
will clearly be more than that, publishing not just course materials but course
frameworks to be linked with local provision. These courses will be tendered
for with staff released on sabbatical to prepare them, and others asked to
independently assess their quality. It also intends to build in regional staff
development to facilitate the use of its materials within institutions' own
courses. If this development achieves anything like its ambitions it will indeed
have a dramatic impact upon part-time and continuing education. By ranging
from access to high level work, it will ease progression. By offering high quality
materials which can be incorporated into existing as well as new local courses
it will influence the nature and structure of full-time courses so that the
traditional division between part- and full-time provision will diminish, and
this may well encourage mixed mode developments. What is more the national
presentation and the distance learning element may well increase the demand
for part-time provision. The prospect of long journeys to college may become
less daunting if there is a powerful distance learning package in support, while,
on the other hand, the prospect of better tutor and student group support may
make the Open University package seem less attractive. On these issues we
can only speculate. What is clear is that the range of combinations of distance
learning and face to face combinations of teaching available to students is
already substantial and is likely to continue to increase.

Performance indicators

The idea of institutions and organizations of any kind identifying goals and
developing criteria of performance should not in itself be controversial.
Performance, if it is to be assessed, can only be assessed adequately in terms of
agreed indicators. Thus the use of 'indicators of some kind in an institution is a
valuable (and well established) part of the management process. Indeed, in
the context of course monitoring and evaluation it is often part of the
self-management process' (Allsop and Findlay 1989). What has made the use
of performance indicators in education controversial has been the lack of
agreed definitions and the particular ways in which they have been applied.
Reviewing much of the literature, Allsop and Findlay (1989) note that
'definition and usage vary widely'. Sometimes the term is used to refer to
simple statistical comparisons, sometimes to the construction of general
indicators and sometimes it is used as part of an attempt to construct precise
measures of performance. It is further complicated in that performance
indicators may be used to evaluate quality of process and sometimes as the
basis for objective comparative analysis.

The term 'performance indicators' has a fairly long history (Birch, Calvert and Sizer 1976). However, Sizer (1989) argues that PIs first came on to the public agenda in the 1980s as a result of the election of the Conservative government in May 1979, with its emphasis upon 'providing value for money in terms of the 3 Es (economy, efficiency and effectiveness)' (Sizer 1989). He identifies the UGC implementation of reductions in recurrent grants to universities as an early example of the use of performance indicators. Although the criteria used were never published, he claims that it is widely assumed that 'A' level scores were used as an input measure of teaching quality (Sizer 1982). This new emphasis on the three Es is also reflected, he argues, in the Jarratt recommendations (see Chapter 2) and in the new contract basis of funding by both PCFC and UFC (see above).

These are all examples of what McVicar and Findlay refer to as the top-down model, which they describe as follows:

> they were mainly designed and implemented by managers or government agencies as part of a control or audit process, were almost exclusively quantitative, expressed as straight student numbers or ratios based on numerical calculations and largely confined to inputs to the educational process.
>
> McVicar and Findlay 1989

This leads to an emphasis upon cost efficiency, which is not the same thing as educational effectiveness. McVicar (1989), drawing on experience of the health service argues that top-down approaches, while they may be valuable in strengthening management control of resources, can have a negative effect upon staff, whose primary concern is quality of service. He argues that a bottom-up approach to performance indicators can usefully address issues of quality and that if there is a future for such indicators in improving educational provision it must be in a combination of top-down and bottom-up approaches. It is this more sophisticated and more complex form of evaluation which Barnett refers to as 'educational audit' (Barnett 1989).

Both models have a significance for and relevance to part-time higher education provision. While most serious commentators reject the narrow view that performance indicators are 'to measure the quality of their output' (HM Inspectors 1989), it is crucial that these performance indicators if they are to be implemented by the funding bodies, do take account of part-time provision. The recent decision to separate part-time from full-time and sandwich provision as a funding category (Chapter 4) suggests some recognition, and so might be seen as a source of encouragement – though it also has its dangers.

Our own research, reported in this book, demonstrates that conventional views of the performance of part-time higher education are false. Part-time provision does not produce poor quality (Chapter 3). It does tend to be institutionally subsidized but only because of the peculiar method of its funding (Chapter 4). When one studies part-time provision in the context of different organizational models of higher education, its performance is impressive (Chapter 5). Top-down performance indicators, even though crude, are capable of offering a direct comparison of part- and full-time modes, which can undermine conventional views of its second rate and peripheral nature and allow proper recognition of its achievements, provided that the appropriate indicators are used. The development of indices of performance more sophisticated than the crude input model favoured by UGC/UFC, raises many of the issues we have discussed throughout this book. One of the great (though probably unintended) achievements of public sector higher education has been the demonstration that input criteria are not a good measure of quality of output (Bourner and Hamed 1987a). This is equally true of part-time provision, which were its performance to be evaluated on value-added criteria would be seen to be impressive indeed.

Bottom-up measures of performance are likely to lead to a further re-evaluation of the utility of part-time provision, though they may also reveal issues of 'quality' of provision. The polytechnics have considerable experience of this form of evaluation through the process of course review. Unfortunately mechanisms have not existed for the wide dissemination of this information so that while some individual institutions have developed sophisticated forms of internal evaluation, 'quality assurance' of this form has not significantly contributed to the national debate. As Allsop and Findlay point out, the PCFC's decision to set up separate working parties on performance indicators and teaching quality does not bode well (Allsop and Findlay 1989).

While we tend to favour Barnett's audit approach we do not intend to attempt to offer a set of performance indicators for part-time provision – though attempts have been made to do this by others (i.e. Warwick University 1987). However, we do wish to stress that supporters of part-time higher education – and continuing education in general – will do themselves no good if they simply reject the performance indicators being developed as crude and incompetent. Once performance indicators are developed by the funding bodies they will form the basis of evaluation for the forseeable future. If appropriate indicators can be developed, which take account of process and output as well as input, we are convinced they will be able to demonstrate the value (and value for money) of part-time provision and the importance of its further future development. The problem of performance indicators for part-time provision is perhaps not so much the effectiveness and efficiency of that provision but the competence and awareness of the evaluators in constructing appropriate criteria.

Conclusions

In developing our model in Chapter 2 we argued that there were political, demographic and economic pressures to reform the system of higher educa-tion. As a consequence policy planning in higher education has begun to place greater importance on attracting a wider range of students into the system, including mature students, those without standard 'A' level entry qualifications, those from lower socio-economic groups, ethnic minorities and part-time students. In the case of part-time students we demonstrated in Chapter 2 that they already constitute a substantial and growing presence in higher education.

In the subsequent chapters we studied the quality of first degree level provision, how it is financed and the organizational arrangements for its delivery. We also considered the consequences of changes in government policy towards higher education. Part-time degree level provision is able to offer wide ranging opportunities to diverse sections of the population. There is no single ideal–typical continuing education student and part-time degree level provision reflects this in offering many different routes. Despite this diversity the quality of service offered is high. Part-time degree provision has also stimulated the development of many innovatory practices in teaching methods, which are now being considered for implementation by the rest of the higher education system.

However, part-time higher education provision has arisen largely from local initiatives and this has limited its impact upon the wider system. Innovatory practices have often not been widely disseminated, even to other part-time degrees, so that part-time provision has remained piecemeal and patchy, responding to local demand when it was identified but rarely seeking to systematically identify potential demand. Furthermore, although the quality of provision overall has been high we found that it varied widely between degrees. Different standards have been deemed to be acceptable in different courses and institutions.

Many difficulties have arisen directly or indirectly from the method of funding part-time provision which we described in Chapter 4. The poor level of funding, especially in the public sector has encouraged departmental fudge and discouraged public debate about efficiency and effectiveness. The irrationalities and inconsistencies of local management practices within the providing institutions often appeared to objectify levels of costs which were a function of the methodology employed as much as any reality. The dominance of the conventional model of higher education has also had consequences for the way in which institutions organize and structure their part-time provision. Different modes of organizing part-time provision appear to have arisen from its supply-led nature. The consequences of this and the internal methods of funding part-time provision for how institutions respond to the government's demand-led philosophy remain to be seen.

Part-time higher education undoubtedly can make a major contribution to the expansion of higher education provision. It already offers an effective service to many of those very types of student that the government wishes to encourage, and it does so without the cost to the government of maintenance grant provision or even the administrative costs implied in a system of student loans. At the same time the introduction of student loans is expected to lead to an increase in the number of full-time students who engage in paid work while they study and so diminish the distinction between full-time and part-time students. Within the providing institutions the development of modularization has also reduced the distinctiveness and separateness of part-time provision. One future role for part-time provision may lie in its closer integration with full-time provision, thus increasing the flexibility of the system as a whole, with students moving from full-time to part-time status as their circumstances alter. However, closer integration may encourage a greater concentration on daytime only part-time provision and so threaten evening only programmes.

Government policy encourages higher participation rates in higher education and claims to recognize the role of part-time provision in this. The introduction of student loans and economic fees have been presented as part of this policy. However, it has been widely claimed that student loans will deter many of the categories of students which the government needs to encourage. At the same time a lack of coherence between educational and social security provision will add to the problems of poorer students. A more flexible part-time alternative might prove attractive in this case but at the moment part-time students are not eligible for student loans so poorer students are unlikely to find the part-time option more attractive. The introduction of economic fees is not intended by the government to militate against part-time students. However, for part-time students taking modules alongside their full-time counterparts on modular degrees this hope becomes unrealistic. The historically low part-time fees in polytechnics and colleges arose from a NAB policy which no longer holds in these market oriented times. The government's own demand-led philosophy requires the providing institutions to seek to charge cost recovering fees. This not only encourages increases of fees on existing part-time programmes but also encourages a different emphasis in new part-time developments. If a key consideration is the level of fee income an emphasis upon employers rather than the students themselves as clients becomes attractive. If this emphasis comes to predominate some traditional types of part-time student may find themselves priced out of the market, while those who remain may see a decline in both the quantity and the quality of what is available at the price. The rise of the employer as client also has implications for changes in the time, content and method of provision.

What we advocate, passionately, is that part-time higher education is taken seriously in policy debate. Higher education has moved a long way from Robbins, when a policy of expansion could assume that part-time provision would eventually wither away. Government ministers now acknowledge the contribution of part-time students to the graduate pool. They congratulate institutions on the success of their part-time programmes. Unfortunately they still fail to address seriously the role that part-time provision has to make to the development of a better educated population. Please do not forget the other routes.

Bibliography

Abramson, M. (1988). 'LINCS: a case study in dynamic networking', *APHE Newsletter*, 2, June.

Allsop, P. and Findlay, P. (1989). 'Performance indicators as an agent of curriculum change: broadening the base of higher education', *Performance Indicators and Quality Control in Higher Education* (1989).

Antill, L. (1986). 'Launching an Open Tech course', *NAFTHE Journal*, 1, February.

Archambault, K. (ed.) (1965). *Philosophical Analyses and Education*. London, Routledge and Kegan Paul.

Association for Part-time Higher Education (1989). 'The Open Polytechnic (2)', *APHE Newsletter*, 4, February.

Bachrach, P. and Baratz, N. S. (1970). *Power and Poverty: Theory and Practice*. London, Oxford University Press.

Bacon, R. and Eltis, W. (1976). *Britain's Economic Problem: Too Few Producers*. London, Macmillan.

Baker, K. (1989a). In a speech reported in *Education Guardian*, 6, January.

Baker, K. (1989b). In a speech reported in *Times Higher Educational Supplement*, 13, January.

Banham, J. (1987). Quoted in *The Observer*, 15 April.

Barnes, A. J. L. and Barr, N. (1988). *Strategy for Higher Education: The Alternative White Paper*. Aberdeen, Aberdeen University Press.

Barnett, C. (1986). *The Audit of War: The Illusion and Reality of Britain as a Great Nation*. London, Macmillan.

Barnett, R. (1986). *Survey of Part-time Degree Course Students' Institutional Provision*. London, CNAA Development Services.

Barnett, R. (1988). 'Entry and exit indicators for higher education: some policy and research issues', *Assessment and Evaluation in Higher Education*, 13, 2.

Barnett, R. (1989). 'Quality control and the development of teaching and learning', in *Performance Indicators and Quality Control in Higher Education* (1989).

Becher, T. (1989). *Academic Tribes and their Territories*. Milton Keynes, Open University Press.

Becher, T. and Kogan, M. (1980). *Process and Structure in Higher Education*. London, Heinemann.

Berg, I. (1973). *Education and Jobs: The Great Training Robbery*. Harmondsworth, Penguin Education.

Bernstein, B. (1971). 'On the classification and framing of educational knowledge', in M. F. D. Young (ed.), *Knowledge and Control*. London, Collier–Macmillan.

Birch, D. W., Calvert, J. R. and Sizer, J. (1976). 'A study of some performance indicators in higher education with particular reference to Lancaster Polytechnic and Loughborough University', *Proceedings of the Third General Conference of Member Institutions*. Paris, 13–16 September.

Birkbeck College (1987). *Birkbeck College: A New Structure*. London, Birkbeck College.

Bosanquet, N. (1983). *After the New Right*. London, Heinemann.

Bourner, T. and Hamed, M. (1987a). *Entry Qualifications and Degree Performance*. London, CNAA Development Services Unit, 10.

Bourner, T. and Hamed, M. (1987b). *Summary Paper*. London, CNAA Development Services Unit, 11.

Boys, C. J., Brennan, J., Henkel, M., Kirkland, J., Kogan, M. and Youill, P. J. (1989). *Higher Education and the Preparation for work*. London, Jessica Kingsley.

Brennan, J. and McGeevor, P. M. (1985). *Higher Education and the Labour Market*. London, CNAA Development Services Unit, 13.

Brennan, J. and McGeevor, P. (1987). *CNAA graduates: Their Employment and Their Experience after Leaving College*. London, CNAA.

Brennan, J. and McGeevor, P. (1988). *Graduates at Work*. London, Jessica Kingsley.

Burgess, T. (1977). *Education after School*. London, Gollancz.

Burnhill, P., Garner, C. and McPherson, A. (1989). *Report* Centre for Educational Research, Edinburgh, University of Edinburgh.

Central Service Unit for Career Services in Universities and Polytechnics (1988). *Annual Report*. London, Central Service Unit for Career Services in Universities and Polytechnics.

Centre for Contemporary Cultural Studies (CCCS) (1981). *Unpopular Education*. London, Hutchinson.

Challis, L. *et al* (1989). *Joint Approaches to Social Policy: Rationality and Practice*. Cambridge, Cambridge University Press.

Claridge, M. (1989). *Wider Access to Higher Education*. Portsmouth, Educational Development Unit, Portsmouth Polytechnic.

Coldstream, P. (1989). 'Conference '89', *APHE Newsletter*, 5, August.

Committee of Vice Chancellors and Principals (CVCP) (1986). *Access and University Courses: Widening Access to Higher Education*. London, CVCP.

Council for Industry and Higher Education (CIHE). (1987). *Towards a Partnership*. London, Council for Industry and Higher Education.

Croham Report (1987). *Review of the University Grants Committee*. Cm 81, London, HMSO.

Crosland, A. (1964). *The Future of Socialism*. London, Cape.

Dale, R. (ed.) (1985). *Education, Training and Employment: Towards a New Vocationalism*. Oxford, Pergamon/Open University.

Dearing, R. (1988). *Address to Planning Conference*. Lancashire Polytechnic, 14 September.

Department of Education and Science (DES) (1985a). *Part-time AFE: An HMI Survey of Vocational Courses*. London, HMSO.

Department of Education and Science (DES) (1985b). *The Development of Higher Education into the 1990s*. Cmnd 9524, London, HMSO.

Department of Education and Science (DES) (1986a). *Projections of Demand for Higher Education in Great Britain 1986–2000*. London, HMSO.

Department of Education and Science (DES). (1986b). *Statistical Bulletin*. 4/86, January.

Department of Education and Science (DES) (1987a). *The Public Expenditure White Paper*. Cmnd 56, London, HMSO.

Department of Education and Science (DES) (1987b). 'International Statistical Comparisons in Higher Education', *Statistical Bulletin*, March.

Department of Education and Science (DES) (1988a). *Statistical Bulletin*. 8/88, June.

Department of Education and Science (DES) (1988b). 'Mature Students in Higher Education', *Statistical Bulletin*, 11.

Department of Education and Science (DES) (1988c). 'Survey of adult education centres in England, 1985–86', *Statistical Bulletin*. 10.

Department of Education and Science (DES) (1988d). *Top-up Loans for Students*. Cmnd 520, London, HMSO.

Department of Education and Science (DES). (1989). *Consultative Document*. April.

Edgley, R. (1978). 'Education for industry', *Radical Philosophy*, Spring.

Times Higher Educational Supplement, Editorial (1988). 'Binary and beyond', 9 September.

Educational Development London Group (1990). *A Directory of Educational Innovations*. London, The London and South-East Regional Polytechnic Consortium for In-Service Training.

Edwards, E. G. (1982). *Higher Education for All*. London, Spokesman.

Edwards Report (1988). *The Future of University Physics*. Report of the Physics Review, University Grants Committee.

Embling, J. (1974). *A Fresh Look at Higher Education*. Amsterdam, Elsevier.

Evans, N. (1984). *Access to Higher Education, Non-standard Entry to CNAA First Degree and DipHe Courses*. London, CNAA Development Services Unit, 6.

Finch, J. (1984). *Education as Social Policy*. Harlow, Longmans.

Finch, J. and Rustin, M. (1986). *The Idea of a Popular University in a Degree of Choice*. Harmondsworth, Penguin.

Fitzgerald, M. (1988). APHE Conference, April 1988, reported in Tight *et al* (1982).

Fulton, O. and Ellwood, S. (1989). *Admissions to Higher Education*. Lancaster University/ Training Agency.

Gallacher, J., Leahy, J. and Sharp, N. (1986). 'Part-time degree students: an initial analysis', *Glasgow College Working Papers in Adult and Continuing Education*, 1.

Gallacher, J., Leahy, J., Sharp, N. and Young, A. (1989). *Part-time Degree Provision in Scotland*. Glasgow College, January.

Gamble, A. (1988). *The Free Economy and the Strong State*. London, Macmillan.

Giroux, H. A. (1983). *Theory and Resistance in Education*. London, Heinemann Educational.

Glennerster, H. (ed.) (1983). *The Future of the Welfare State: Remaking Social Policy*. London, Heinemann.

Glennerster, H. and LeGrand, J. (1984). 'Student loans or graduate tax', *New Society*, December.

Goldman, D., Saunders, M. and Smith, D. M. (1989). 'Meeting with Robert Jackson', *APHE Newsletter*, 5, July.

Gow, D. and Weston, C. (1989). 'University shake-up underway', *Guardian*, 28 March.

Gray, J. *et al* (1983). *Reconstructions of Secondary Education*. London, Routledge and Kegan Paul.

Halsey, A. H. (1987). 'Who owns the curriculum of higher education?', *Journal of Educational Policy*, 2, 4.

Halsey, A. H., Heath, A. and Ridge, J. (1980). *Origins and Destinations*. Oxford, Clarendon Press.

Hargreaves, D. (1982). *The Challenge of the Comprehensive School*. London, Routledge and Kegan Paul.

Heald, D. (1983). *Public Expenditure*. Oxford, Martin Robertson.

Her Majesty's Senior Inspector of Schools (1989). *Standards in Education 1988–89*. London, HMSO.

Hilton, A. (1989). 'The consortia approach', *SEEC News*, 1 January.

Hirst, P. H. (1965). 'Liberal education and the nature of knowledge', in Archambault (1965).

Hirst, P. H. and Peters, R. S. (1970). *The Logic of Education*. London, Routledge and Kegan Paul.

HMSO (1989). *Autumn Statement*.

Hoare, Q. (1965). 'Education: programmes and men' *New Left Review*, 32.

Hogwood, B. W. and Gunn, L. A. (1984). *Policy Analysis for the Real World*. London, Oxford University Press.

Holmberg, B. (1985). *On the Status of Distance Education in the World in the 1980s*. Fernuniversitat, Hagen, West Germany.

Hussain, A. (1976). 'The relationship between education and the economy', *Economy and Society*, 5, 1.

Illich, I. (1971). *Deschooling Society*. London, Calder and Boyars.

Institute of Manpower Studies (IMS) (1988). *IMS Supplement*. Brighton, Institute of Manpower Studies, June.

Jarratt Report (1985). *Report of the Steering Committee for Efficiency Studies in Universities*. Committee of Vice-Chancellors and Principals.

Jarvis, P, (1981). 'The Open University unit: androgy or pedagogy?', *Teaching at a Distance*, 20.

Jarvis, P. (1983). *Adult and Continuing Education: Theory and Practice*. London, Croom Helm.

Jarvis, P. (1985). *The Sociology of Adult and Continuing Education*. London, Croom Helm.

Jarvis, P. (1989). *Adult Learners in the Social Context*. London, Croom Helm.

Johnes, J. and Taylor, J. (1989). 'Undergraduate non-completion rates: differences between UK universities', *Higher Education*, 18, 3.

Johnson, R. W. (1989). *New Statesman and New Society*, 29 September.

Johnson, S. and Hall, R. (1985). *A Hard Day's Night*. London, Polytechnic of Central London.

Jones, P. and Killoh, J. (1987). 'The management of the polytechnics', in Becher (1987).

Kail, L. J. (1988). *Financial Devolution: Departmental Cost Centres and Incentives*. Guildford, University of Surrey.

Kelly, T. (1970). *A History of Adult Education in Great Britain from the Middle Ages to the Twentieth Century*. Liverpool, Liverpool University Press.

Kidourie, E. (1989). *Perestroika in the Universities*. London, Institute of Economic Affairs.

Knowles, M. S. (1978). *The Modern Practice of Adult Education*. Chicago, Association Press.

Kogan, M. (1986). *Education Accountability*. London, Hutchinson.

Kogan, M. and Kogan, D. (1983). *The Attack on Higher Education*. London, Kogan Page.

Lacey, C. (1970). *Hightown Grammer*. Manchester, Manchester University Press.

Laidlaw, B. and Layard, R. (1974). 'Traditional versus Open University teaching methods: a cost comparison', *Higher Education*, 3.

Laslett, P. (1989). *A Fresh Map of Life*. London, Weidenfeld.

Lawson, K. H. (1982). *Analysis and Ideology: Conceptual Essays on the Education of Adults*. Nottingham, The University Department of Adult Education.

LeGrand, J. and Robinson, R. (1984). *Privatization and the Welfare State*. London, George and Allen and Unwin.

Lindop, N. (1987). Speech, *Access Conference*, Polytechnic of North London, February.

Lewis, R. with MacDonald, L. (1988). *The Open Learning Pocket Workbook*. National Council for Educational Technology (NCET).

Lindsay, R. O. and Paton-Salzberg, R. (1987). 'Resource changes and academic performance at an English polytechnic', *Studies in Higher Education*, 12, 2.

Lockwood, G. (1985a). 'Universities as organizations', in Lockwood and Davis (1985b).

Lockwood, G. (1987). 'The management of universities', in Becher (1987).

Lockwood, G. and Davis, J. (1985b). *Universities: the Management Challenge*. Windsor, Berks, SRHE/NFER Nelson.

Mace, J. (1989). 'The demand for higher education', *Higher Education Review*, 21, 2.

Marquand, D. (1988). *The Unprincipled Society*. London, Fontana.

Marris, R. (1983). *Birkbeck College Discussion Paper*. London, Birkbeck College.

Marsland, D. (1988). *Seeds of Bankruptcy: Sociological Bias against Business and Freedom*. London, Claridge.

Muta, H. (1985). 'The economics of the university of the air in Japan', *Higher Education*, 14.

MacGregor, J. (1989a). Reported in *Financial Times*, 16 November.

MacGregor, J. (1989b). Reported in *Times Higher Educational Supplement*, 29 September.

McVicar, M. (1989). 'Performance indicators in quality assurance: what can we learn from the NHS?', in *Performance Indicators and Quality Control in Higher Education* (1989).

McVicar, M. and Findlay, P. (1989). Introduction, in *Performance Indicators and Quality Control in Higher Education* (1989).

National Advisory Body/University Grants Committee (NAB/UGC) Continuing Education Standing Committee (1988a). *Return to Study*. London, NAB/UGC.

National Advisory Body/University Grants Committee (NAB/UGC) Continuing Education Standing Committee (1988b). *Credit Where Credit's Due*. London, NAB/UGC.

National Association of Teachers in Further and Higher Education (NATFHE) (undated). 'Association comments on the DES Consultative Document: contracts between the funding bodies and higher education institutions', *NATFHE Briefing Document*, 3.

National Association of Teachers in Further and Higher Education (NATFHE) (1989). *'Statistical report'*, *NATFHE Journal*, Summer.

National Association of Teachers in Further and Higher Education (NATFHE) (1988). 'What will the Bill proposals do to adult education?', *NATFHE Journal*, Extra.

National Institute of Adult and Continuing Education (NIACE) (1989). *Adults in Higher Education*. London, National Institute of Adult and Continuing Education.

Observer, the (1989), article, 5 November.

O'Hear, A. (1988). 'Academic freedom and the university', in Tight (1988).

O'Leary, J. (1987). 'Review of the White Paper', *Times Higher Educational Supplement*, 10 April.

Oleson, V. L. and Whittaker, E. W. (1968). *The Silent Dialogue: A Study in the Social Psychology of Professional Socialization.* San Francisco, Jossey-Bass.

P. A. Consulting Group (1989). Reported in the *Observer*, 6 January.

Patterson, R. W. K. (1984). 'Objectivity as an educational imperative', *International Journal of Lifelong Education*, 3.

Pearson, R. and Pike, G. (1989a). *The Graduate Labour Market in the 1990s.* Institute of Manpower Studies, Falmer, Sussex, IMS Report 167.

Pearson, R. and Pike, G. (1989b). *How Many Graduates in the 21st Century? The Choice is Yours.* Institute of Manpower Studies. Falmer, Sussex, IMS Report 177.

Performance Indicators and Quality Control in Higher Education (1989). Papers presented to a conference at Institute of Education, University of London, 27 September 1989. Portsmouth, Portsmouth Polytechnic.

Phillips, M., Huhne, C. and Fairhall, D. (1989). 'How the cards are stacked', the *Guardian*, 15 March.

Pollard, D. (1989). Conference presentation, *APHE Conference*, May, London.

Pollitt, C. (1990). 'Measuring university performance: never mind the quality, never mind the width', *Higher Education Quarterly*, 44, 1.

Polytechnic and Colleges Funding Council (PCFC) (1989a). *Funding Choices: Methods of Funding Higher Education in Polytechnics and Colleges.* PCFC Consultative Document, March.

Polytechnic and Colleges Funding Council (PCFC) (1989b). *Recurrent Funding Methodology*, PCFC Consultative Committee.

Portwood, D. (1988). 'Associate student and credit accumulation and transfer schemes'. *South East England Consortia (SEEC)*, October.

Pratt, J. and Burgess, T. (1974). London, Routledge and Kegan Paul.

Purvis, J. and Hales, M. (eds) (1983). *Achievement and Inequality in Education.* London, Routledge and Kegan Paul.

Rehn, G. Paris, (1972). *Prospective View of Patterns of Time Working.* Paris, United Nations Organization for Economic Cooperation and Development (OECD).

Richards, M. (1988). 'Open Poly plans for mass access', *Times Higher Educational Supplement*, 29 April.

Rickett, R. (1987). Quoted in the *Observer*, 5 April.

Robbins, L., Lord. (1963). *Students and Their Higher Education: Report of the Committee on Higher Education 1961–63.* London, HMSO.

Roberts, D. (1988). Conference presentation. *PACE Conference* 1988, Wolverhampton.

Robinson, E. (1968). *The New Polytechnics.* Harmondsworth, Penguin.

Robinson, E. (1988a). APHE Conference, reported in Tight *et al* (1988).

Robinson, E. (1988b). 'The polytechnics: 20 years of 'social control', *Higher Education Review*, 20, 2.

Rumble, G. (1980). *The Planning and Management of Distance Education.* London, Croom Helm.

Rustin, M. (1986). 'The idea of a popular university', in Finch and Rustin (1986).

Salter, B. and Tapper, T. (1981). *Education, Politics and the State.* London, Grant McIntyre.

Saunders, M. R. and Smith, D. M. (1989). 'Post-graduate part-time students', *APHE Newsletter*, November.

Schools Examinations Council (SEC) (1988). 'Approval of GCSE syllabuses', *SEC News*, 9, Summer.

Segal, A. (1989). 'Courses guide', the *Guardian*, 7 February.

Sizer, J. (1982). 'Assessing institutional performance and progress', in *L Wagner* (1982).

Sizer, J. (1989). 'Performance indicators, quality control and the maintenance of standards in higher education', in *Performance Indicators and Quality Control in Higher Education* (1989).

Smith, D. M. (1968). *Mass Communication in its Social Context.* MA thesis, University of Exeter.

Smith, D. M. and Saunders, M. R. (1988). 'Part-time higher education: prospects and practices', *Higher Education Review*, 20, 3.

Smith, D. M. and Saunders, M. R. (1989a). *Part-time Higher Education: Policy and Practice.* A report for CNAA development Services, London, CNAA.

Smith, D. M. and Saunders, M. R. (1989b). 'Reflections on the White Paper', *APHE Newsletter*, 4, February.

Smithers, A. and Robinson, P. (1989). *Increasing Participation in Higher Education.* Manchester, University of Manchester Press.

Social Trends (1988). London, HMSO.

Social Trends (1989). London, HMSO.

Sofer, A. (1988). Agenda. *Education Guardian*, 6 July.

Squires, G. (1990). *First Degree: The Undergraduate Curriculum.* Society for Research into Higher Education (SRHE) / Open University.

Statistical Report (1988). *Training Skills Bulletin*, 5.

Stone Report (1988). *University Chemistry: The Way Forward.* Report of the Chemistry Review, University Grants Committee.

Tarsh, J. (1987), 'Subject to demand', *Times Higher Educational Supplement.* 26 June.

Tight, M. (1982). *Part-time degree level study in the United Kingdom.* London, Advisory Council for Adult and Continuing Education.

Tight, M. (1986). *Part-time degrees, diplomas and certificates.* Cambridge, Hobson's Choice.

Tight, M. (1988). *Academic Freedom and Responsibility.* Milton Keynes, SRHE/Open University Press.

Tight, M. (1990). *Part-time degrees, diplomas and certificates.* CRAC/Hobsons Publishing.

Tight, M. (1987). 'The value of higher education: full-time or part-time?', *Studies in Higher Education*, 12, 2.

Tight, M., Bishop, R., Hanson, A., Saunders, M. R., Sharp, N. and Smith, D. M. (1988). 'Resourcing part-time HE: a report on the APHE conference held 25 April 1988', *APHE Newsletter*, 2, June.

Times Higher Educational Supplement (1988). 'The same differences', 9 September.

Times Higher Educational Supplement (1989). Report, 19 May.

Tribe, K. (1990). 'The accumulation of cultural capital: the funding of UK higher education in the twentieth century', *Higher Education Quarterly*, 44, 1.

Trow, M. (1989). 'The Robbins trap: British attitudes and the levels of expansion', *Higher Education Quarterly*, 43, 1.

Trow, M. (1988). Quoted in *Times Higher Educational Supplement*, 8 July.

UCCA (1988). *Press release.* Universities Central Clearing Admissions, December.

Universities Council for Adult and Continuing Education (1990). *Report of the Working Party on Part-time Degrees.* Occasional Paper No 1. Warwick, University of Warwick.

UDACE (1988a). *Adults and the Act: The Education Reform Act 1988 and Adult Learners.* Leicester, Unit for the Development of Adult Continuing Education.

UDACE (1988b). *Developing Access: The Discussion Paper.* Leicester, Unit for the Development of Adult Continuing Education.

Universities Funding Council (UFC) (1989). *Circular Letter*, 19 May.

Vaizey, J. (1962). *The Economics of Education*. London, Faber.

Wagner, L. (1977). 'The Economics of the Open University revisited', *Higher Education*, 6.

Wagner, L. (ed.) (1982). *Agenda for Institutional Change in Higher Education*. Guildford, SRHE, Monograph 45.

Walker, S. and Barton, L. (eds) (1984). *Social Crisis and Educational Research*. London, Croom Helm.

Warnock, M. (1989). *Knowing our Minds*. Counterblast 8, London, Chatto.

Warwick University, Department of Continuing Education (1987). *Towards a Continuing Education Audit: Warwick Indicators for Performance Measurement*. Coventry, University of Warwick.

Weekend Guardian (1989) 7 January.

Weiner, M. J. (1981). *English Culture and the Decline of the Industrial Spirit, 1950–1980*. Cambridge, Cambridge University Press.

Wilding, P. (ed.) (1987). *In Defence of the Welfare State*. Manchester, Manchester University Press.

Williams, G. and Blackstone, T. (1983). *Response to Adversity: Higher Education in a Harsh Climate*. Leverhulme 10, SRHE/Leverhulme.

Williamson, B. (1990). *Times Higher Educational Supplement*. 13 April.

Willis, P. (1977). *Learning to Labour: How Working Class Kids get Working Class Jobs*. Farnborough, Saxon House.

Wright, P. (1989). 'Access or exclusion: some comments and future prospects of continuing education in England', *Studies in Higher Education*, 14, 1.

Young, M. F. D. (1971). *Knowledge and Control*. London, Collier-Macmillan.

Index

The Society for Research into Higher Education

The Society exists both to encourage and co-ordinate research and development into all aspects of Higher Education; including academic, organizational and policy issues; and also to provide a forum for debate, verbal and printed.

The Society's income derives from subscriptions, book sales, conference fees, and grants. It receives no subsidies and is wholly independent. Its corporate members are institutions of higher education, research institutions and professional, industrial, and governmental bodies. Its individual members include teachers and researchers, administrators and students. Members are found in all parts of the world and the Society regards its international work as amongst its most important activities.

The Society is opposed to discrimination in higher education on grounds of belief, race, etc.

The Society discusses and comments on policy, organizes conferences, and encourages research. It is studying means of preserving archives of higher education. Under the imprint SRHE & OPEN UNIVERSITY PRESS it is a specialist publisher of research, having some 30 titles in print. The Editorial Board of the Society's Imprint seeks authoritative research or study in the field. It offers competitive royalties; a highly recognizable format in both hard- and paper-back; and the world-wide reputation of the Open University Press. The Society also publishes *Studies in Higher Education* (three times a year), which is mainly concerned with academic issues; *Higher Education Quarterly* (formerly *Universities Quarterly*), mainly concerned with policy issues; *Abstracts* (three times a year); an *International Newsletter* (twice a year) and *S.R.H.E. NEWS* (four times a year).

The Society's Committees, Study Groups and Branches are run by members (with help from a small secretariat at Guildford). The Groups at present include a Teacher Education Study Group, a Staff Development Group, a Continuing Education Group, a Women in Higher Education Group and an Excellence in Teaching Group. The Groups may have their own organization, subscriptions, or publications; (e.g. the *Staff Development Newsletter*). A further *Question of Quality* Group has organized a series of Anglo-American seminars in the USA and the UK.

The Society's annual conferences are held jointly; 'Access & Institutional Change' (1989, with the Polytechnic of North London). In 1990, the topic will be 'Industry and Higher Education' (with the University of Surrey). In 1991, the topic will be 'Research and Higher Education', with the University of Leicester: in 1992, it will be 'Learning & Teaching' (with Nottingham Polytechnic). In 1993, the topic will be 'Governments, Higher Education and Accountability'. Other conferences have considered the 'HE After the Election' (1987) and 'After the Reform Act' (July 1988).

Members receive free of charge the Society's *Abstracts*, annual conference Proceedings, (or 'Precedings'), *S.R.H.E. News* and *International Newsletter*. They may buy *SRHE & Open University Press* books at 35 per cent discount, and *Higher Education Quarterly* on special terms. Corporate members also receive the Society's journal *Studies in Higher Education* free; (individuals on special terms). Members may also obtain certain other journals at a discount, including the NFER *Register of Educational Research*. There is a substantial discount to members, and to staff of corporate members, on annual and some other conference fees. The discounts can exceed the subscription.

		Annual Subscriptions
		August 1990–July 1991
Individual members		£43.00
Students & retired members		£12.00
Hardship		£20.00
Corporate members		
less than 1000 students		£155.00
1000–3000 students		£195.00
more than 3000 students		£290.00
Non-teaching bodies	up to	£295.00

Further information: SRHE at the University, Guildford GU2 5XH, UK Tel: (0483) 39003 Fax: (0483) 300903
Catalogue: *SRHE & Open University Press*, Celtic Court, 22 Ballmoor, Buckingham MK18 1XW. Tel: (0280) 823388